Francis Robert Beattie

Radical Criticism

an exposition and examination of the radical critical theory concerning the

literature and religious system of the Old Testament scriptures

Francis Robert Beattie

Radical Criticism
an exposition and examination of the radical critical theory concerning the literature and religious system of the Old Testament scriptures

ISBN/EAN: 9783337264307

Printed in Europe, USA, Canada, Australia, Japan

Cover: Foto ©Lupo / pixelio.de

More available books at **www.hansebooks.com**

RADICAL CRITICISM

RADICAL CRITICISM

AN EXPOSITION AND EXAMINATION OF THE RADICAL
CRITICAL THEORY CONCERNING THE LITERA-
TURE AND RELIGIOUS SYSTEM OF THE
OLD TESTAMENT SCRIPTURES

BY

FRANCIS R. BEATTIE

PROFESSOR OF SYSTEMATIC THEOLOGY AND APOLOGETICS IN THE LOUISVILLE
PRESBYTERIAN THEOLOGICAL SEMINARY, AND AUTHOR OF "AN EXAMI-
NATION OF UTILITARIANISM" AND "THE METHODS OF THEISM"

WITH AN INTRODUCTION BY

W. W. MOORE, D.D., LL.D.

PROFESSOR OF OLD TESTAMENT LITERATURE IN UNION THEOLOGICAL
SEMINARY, VIRGINIA

FLEMING H. REVELL COMPANY
CHICAGO : : : NEW YORK : : : TORONTO
Publishers of Evangelical Literature

Entered according to Act of Congress, in the year 1894, by

FLEMING H. REVELL COMPANY,

In the Office of the Librarian of Congress at Washington, D. C.

INTRODUCTION.

BY PROFESSOR W. W. MOORE, D. D., LL. D., VIRGINIA.

THE science of Biblical Criticism falls naturally into three main divisions; viz., the Lower Criticism, which is concerned with the accuracy of the biblical text; the Higher Criticism, which is concerned with the age and character of the biblical books; and the Exegetical Criticism, which is concerned with the meaning of the biblical statements. As the Exegetical Criticism has for its end the ascertaining of the meaning of Scripture by the various processes of interpretation, and as the Lower Criticism has for its task the determination of the exact words of Scripture in the original by comparison of manuscripts and other processes, so the Higher Criticism has for its task the settlement of all questions pertaining to the age, authorship, structure, and trustworthiness of the various books of Scripture by a study of their literary phenomena and their historical and theological contents. In other words, criticism is investigation; and the criticism of contents is no less necessary than the criticism of text or of interpretation. Hence Dr. Beattie's frequent and hearty commendation of the Higher Criticism, properly defined as a searching examination of the form and the facts of Holy Scripture. Hence also Professor Mead's emphatic assertion: "I regard the Higher Criticism as not only legitimate, but as very useful, and indiscriminate condemnation of it as foolish. Genuine criticism is nothing but the search after truth ; and of this there cannot be too much."

But, as the Lower Criticism has been abused by those who have insisted upon radical reconstructions of the Hebrew text, and as the Exegetical Criticism has been abused by those who have propounded false theories of interpretation, from the days of the Talmudists down to the present time, so the Higher Criticism has been abused by those who have engaged in wild speculation concerning the history, literature, and religion of the ancient Hebrews. It is against the abuse of this science that Dr. Beattie's book is directed, as the title of the work itself indicates. He sees the gravity of the issue ; he knows that "the assaults of Colenso, Kuenen, and Wellhausen are delivered against the central keep of Protestantism, — the supreme authority of the Bible in matters of religion." And yet he avoids both of the mistakes into which so many conservative writers of less learning and ability have fallen. In the first place, he does not commit the blunder of conceding that the rationalists are the only scientific students of Scripture, by permitting them to monopolize the name of "higher critics." The popular misconception of this title, by which it is made to mean superior critics, and which implies that all who bear it are arrogant and supercilious as well as hostile to the Bible, is indeed widespread even among ministers. But there is all the more reason to correct this impression, though it undoubtedly requires courage to do it, and to make it clear that the term "Higher Criticism" has a well-established meaning among biblical scholars, having been so called for the simple reason that "the study of the contents of a book will always be considered a higher study than that of the words in which those contents are expressed." In the second place, Dr. Beattie does not rely upon hysterical vituperation and indiscriminate abuse of the men whose views he combats, but upon clear definition, and solid argument, and Holy Scripture. It has made us sick at heart to observe how many of those who have undertaken to speak in the popular periodicals for the conservative side in this controversy have, by their want of discrimination and their violent and abusive tone, injured our cause and fostered a timorous view of truth. *Non tali auxilio nec defensoribus istis.*

The manner in which our author handles this difficult and exciting subject is very different. While he is absolutely uncompromising in his opposition to the errors of a destructive criticism, his tone is not that of a man who is trembling for the ark; but rather that of one who knows whereof he speaks and why he maintains the old views concerning the integrity, authorship, and date of the various portions of the Bible; and we venture the assertion that his discriminating and dignified discussion will do more good among intelligent people than all the objurgation and rhodomontade of our slashing sciolists old and young combined. There is earnest work to be done in the battle with those radical critics who are threatening the foundations of our faith, and it is refreshing to see a man enter this conflict who appreciates the gravity of the crisis, who possesses the requisite equipment, and who knows the true method of our defense.

There is urgent need of such work as this just now. The aggressiveness of the negative critics and the fascinating presentation of their views in various popular journals make it the duty of conservative scholars to put all the facts within the reach of the general reader. Dr. Beattie's book is sound, timely, and readable. May the God of truth prosper this enlightened endeavor to confirm the faith of the people in his infallible word.

PREFACE.

THE substance of this little treatise appeared during the past year as a series of articles in the *Christian Observer*. These articles are now issued in a permanent form in response to the expressed desire of friends whose favorable judgment the writer values very highly. They are published with some necessary verbal corrections, and a few additions are made at important points in the discussion. The arrangement of the articles is slightly changed, and a table of contents is added.

It is proper to say that these articles do not profess to be either a technical or a complete discussion of the important subject with which they deal. They were originally intended for the general readers of a weekly religious newspaper, rather than for any scholarly circle. This accounts for the somewhat popular form into which the discussion is cast, and which it has been deemed best to retain. In this form it is hoped that the articles may give to that class of earnest minds, who desire a popular rather than a technical treatment of the Higher Criticism, an intelligible view of a subject which excites so much interest at the present day.

That such a popular discussion of this subject is needful is evident from the fact that certain methods of historical criticism which may justly be termed *destructive* are now set forth in various attractive and popular forms. It has passed from the study of the scholar to the circle of the general reader. It no longer speaks only in technical terms, but expresses itself in the language of the common people. If this destructive criticism be dangerous as thus presented, an exhibition of its serious defects, in as simple terms as possible, may serve a useful purpose.

Another thing is also aimed at in this treatise. Care has been taken to point out that the questions raised by the Higher Criticism are proper matters of study at the hands of biblical scholars. It is claimed that in dealing with these questions there are legitimate and illegitimate methods of procedure. An attempt is made to exhibit the former, and to utter a warning against the latter. This little book, therefore, is not an assault upon the reverent Higher Criticism of the Scriptures, but upon the illegitimate methods, and destructive results of a certain class of modern critics. In exposing the false we conserve the true in biblical study. This work is now sent forth with the earnest prayer that it may serve the interests of the truth, and be for the honor of the Master.   FRANCIS R. BEATTIE.

Louisville, January, 1895.

CONTENTS.

PART I.—INTRODUCTORY.

CHAPTER I.

PRELIMINARY 21
Importance of the subject—The nature of the discussion—The popular attention arrested—Earnestness in advocacy of certain views.

CHAPTER II.

HIGHER CRITICISM DEFINED 27
Biblical Criticism defined—Textual or Lower Criticism described—Higher or Historical Criticism described—Its sphere.

CHAPTER III.

RADICAL HIGHER CRITICISM DEFINED . . . 34
Difficult to define—Various names given to it—Matter of method, attitude, and standpoint—Its bearing on the supernatural.

PART II.—HISTORY OF THE CRITICAL MOVEMENT.

CHAPTER I.

ITS HISTORY 43
Early stages—Porphyry—Spinoza—Relation to pantheism—Simon—Clericus.

CHAPTER II.

Its History Continued 49

English deism — Collins — Jean Astruc — His conjectures — Raised difficulties — Transition to Germany.

CHAPTER III.

Its History Continued 55

De Wette and Paulus — Vatke and George — Reuss — Hegel's philosophy — Strauss.

CHAPTER IV.

Its History Continued 61

The Tübingen School — Baur and Tendency Theory — Graf — Kuenen — Wellhausen.

CHAPTER V.

Its History Concluded 68

Robertson Smith — Transition to Britain — Toy — Briggs — Driver and Cheyne — Harper — Conservatives: Ranke, Kurtz, Hengstenberg, König, Klostermann, Watts, Green, Osgood, Bissell, Warfield.

PART III. — Exposition of Radical Higher Criticism.

CHAPTER I.

Preliminary 79

Higher Criticism began without the Church — But in modern times is within it — Warning — False theories slowly mature results — No objection to legitimate Higher Criticism — Practical considerations.

CHAPTER II.

PHILOSOPHICAL PRESUPPOSITIONS 87

A caution — Import of the philosophy held — The Hegelian philosophy — Pantheism again — The supernatural ignored or rejected — Kuenen.

CHAPTER III.

PHILOSOPHICAL PRESUPPOSITIONS CONTINUED . . 95

Relation of Higher Criticism to inspiration — Radical Criticism rejects or reconstructs the doctrine — Some seek to hold sound views — Three positions stated — Natural evolution the fourth philosophical presupposition.

CHAPTER IV.

THE METHODS OF ADVANCED CRITICISM . . . 103

Theoretical nature of these methods — A theory as to the national life of Israel — As to the religious system — And as to the sacred literature of that system.

CHAPTER V.

THE DOCUMENTARY HYPOTHESIS 112

The Hypothesis explained — Various symbols described — How applied to explain the production of the Scriptures.

CHAPTER VI.

THE THREE CODES 122

The theory of the Codes explained — Covenant Code — Deuteronomic Code — Priestly or Levitical Code — The Law of holiness.

CHAPTER VII.

SOME GENERAL FEATURES 130
Reconstruction by means of the Codes — Features of the literature — The era of Josiah — The period of Ezra — Ezekiel — The Tabernacle idea.

CHAPTER VIII.

THE HISTORY 138
The history and the ritual — The prophetical and the priestly lines — The origin, codification, and writing of laws — Traditional explanations — Fictitious theory — Pseudonymous authorship.

CHAPTER IX.

THE PROPHETS AND THE PSALMS 146
The prophets and the law — Not the law and the prophets — Writing prophets early — Hosea, Jonah, and Amos — Isaiah — The law and ritual post-prophetic — Psalms largely post-exilic and non-Davidic also — Import of this.

PART IV.— CRITICAL EXAMINATION.

CHAPTER I.

PRELIMINARY 157
The present current debate of vital importance — Questions lie deeper than mere authorship and literary style — The nature of the religion of the Scriptures involved — No assumptions allowed — No safe middle course in the controversy — Conservative criticism has an important task.

CHAPTER II.

THE UNDERLYING PHILOSOPHY 165

The underlying philosophy criticised — Whether deistic or pantheistic, defective — Bearing on inspiration considered — No really inspired Scriptures — Higher Criticism subjective in its radical phases.

CHAPTER III.

ITS PHILOSOPHY OF RELIGION 174

Naturalistic Evolution cannot explain all religion — Comparative Religion — A mere assumption — Factors in Christianity not in other religions — Advance not accounted for — Law of natural progress is Degeneration.

CHAPTER IV.

GENERAL HISTORICAL DEFECTS 183

History gives important tests — Historicity of the Scriptures — Each age presupposes the previous age — Silence regarding any observance does not prove non-existence — No good account given of the revolt of the ten tribes by radical critics — Other important historical matters.

CHAPTER V.

PARTICULAR HISTORICAL DEFECTS 192

Testimony of Josephus — Historic setting of the Law — Looks back to Egypt and forward to Canaan — Reform under Josiah and the restoration under Ezra not well explained — Choice of a king — Amalekites — Attempts to explain away fail.

CHAPTER VI.

THE DOCUMENTARY HYPOTHESIS 201
Hypothesis had a doubtful origin — Astruc — Too much stress laid upon the documents — Radical Critics superficial — The hypothesis cannot now be proved — Names "Jehovah" and "Elohim" explained — Destroys the organic unity of Scripture.

CHAPTER VII.

THE THREE CODES 210
Proof of the codes needed — Not necessarily successive — Lack of agreement as to the order of the Codes — Can trace the Priestly Code back to the Conquest — Why all ascribed to Moses?

CHAPTER VIII.

DEUTERONOMY 218
This the great test — Mosaic origin natural — Laws in Deuteronomy what we would expect — Silence proves nothing — Deuteronomy not first to enjoin worship at one sanctuary — Its unity — Can trace Deuteronomy back to the days of the Conquest.

CHAPTER IX.

THE GRADED PRIESTHOOD . . . , . 226
Three grades — So from the first — Deuteronomy — Special provision made for the support of Levites — Historical books prove three orders from the first — Tabernacle implied the three orders.

CHAPTER X.

THE TABERNACLE 234
Explanations of Radical Criticism far-fetched — Tabernacle suited for wilderness — Late origin confusing — No use after the Exile — History proves early existence — Import of all this.

CHAPTER XI.

THE GREAT FEASTS 242

The great feasts described — Not nature festivals — True view of the feasts — Silence proves nothing — Time set for feasts — Purpose of the feasts perverted — History proves early existence of the feasts.

CHAPTER XII.

THE PROPHETS 250

The Radical Critics minimize prophecy — No proof of the inversion of the order of the law and prophets — Silence — Natural development, if admitted, proves too much — The prophets often call the people back to a neglected law — Prophets allude to the Exodus in a way which tells against Radical Criticism — Prophets did not originate ethic monotheism — Advanced ideas.

CHAPTER XIII.

THE PSALMS 258

Psalms not merely the praise-book of the second temple — Davidic authorship of many of the Psalms not disproved — History alluded to in the Psalms — The religious ideas of the Psalms in harmony with that age — Not post-exilic in spirit — Teach monotheism — Presuppose the law.

CHAPTER XIV.

THE GOSPEL NARRATIVES 267

Import of this topic — Gospel history refutes — Ascribe Mosaic origin to the law — Also the priestly system — Bearing on Isaiah — Radical Criticism signally fails on this field — Kenosis.

CHAPTER XV.

OTHER NEW TESTAMENT BOOKS 276

Wide field — Acts — Romans — Galatians — Hebrews — All agree with the views of Conservative Criticism.

CHAPTER XVI.

DOCTRINAL CONSIDERATIONS 286

Dogmatics and Exegesis — Breaks unity of Scripture — Recasts inspiration — Old Testament doctrine of Christ impugned — Redemptive doctrines affected — Work of Holy Spirit impaired.

CHAPTER XVII.

THE EVIDENCE OF ARCHÆOLOGY 294

Highly important — Destroys mythical theory — Confirms history — This establishes Mosaic origin of law — Proves early origin of writing — Shows high civilization in early times — Names given.

CHAPTER XVIII.

SUMMARY 305

The history, the exposition, and the main results of the Criticism summarized.

CHAPTER XIX.

CONCLUDING REMARKS , ... 314

Legitimate Higher Criticism useful — Illegitimate baneful — Claims of radical critics arrogant — Present status of the controversy estimated — Final outcome not doubtful — The spirit and methods of radical criticism dangerous to evangelical views of truth — Higher Criticism and our standards — A challenge — Conclusion.

PART I.

INTRODUCTORY.

CHAPTER I.

PRELIMINARY.

IN a few brief chapters, it is our purpose to discuss, in a somewhat popular way, some of the principles, methods, and results of modern *advanced* Higher Criticism of the sacred Scriptures, and of the proposed reconstructions of the religious system which they contain. Most of our readers have heard more or less of the Higher Criticism, and yet it may be safely assumed that not very many have clear views in regard to what it really is. Perhaps fewer still understand the distinction between a sound and legitimate treatment of the questions which properly belong to Higher Criticism, and a false and illegitimate procedure which may be followed in dealing with these questions. We trust that a brief treatise, written in a somewhat popular manner, may enable our readers to form more definite opinions in regard to some things that are at best vague and ill-defined even in many intelligent minds. Above all, we earnestly hope that what we shall say may minister to the confirmation of the faith of all our readers in the sacred Scriptures as the inspired word of God, and in the divinity of the redemptive scheme which they unfold through Jesus Christ, the Son of God and Saviour of men. This chapter will be introductory in its nature.

Biblical studies have always possessed deep interest for thoughtful minds. The sacred literature of the Christian system, in its origin, contents and purpose, has engaged more earnest and scholarly attention than any other literature in the world. We see this interest in all the ages. The Jewish Rabbis, the Christian Fathers, and mediæval Scholastics illustrate in various ways this interest and attention. Since the Reformation, biblical studies have been diligently pursued, and at the present day the devotion to these studies is extensive and ardent. The number of books that are published annually, dealing directly or indirectly with biblical topics, is full proof of this statement, and this fact constitutes one of the hopeful signs of the times.

At the present day, the questions most debated are critical, rather than dogmatic, in their nature. The discussions are literary, rather than doctrinal; historical, rather than theological. Soon after the rise of the modern school of literary and historical criticism, less than a century ago, we find that its principles and methods were applied to the sacred Scriptures. The books of the Bible were subjected to rigid scrutiny, and the results reached in certain quarters were startling. In the earlier decades of the present century, rationalistic criticism in Germany in the hands of men like Paulus, Eichhorn,

Semler, and De Wette, made sad havoc with the narratives of the Scriptures, and paved the way for the mythical theories of Vatke and Strauss in regard to the Old and New Testaments respectively.

During the past decade or two, more cautious, though scarcely less destructive, criticism has prevailed extensively in certain quarters, and the Scriptures have been subjected to patient investigation and almost painfully microscopic inspection. Again and again the sacred records have refused to yield to the assaults made on them, or to melt away in the critic's crucible. As to the widespread prevalence of this school of criticism, there can be no doubt, and we would be unwise not to seek to understand its import. Still we need have no fear as to the outcome of the conflict. As the oak upon the mountain side, swept by many a stormy gale, has its roots made the stronger, and its fiber knit the firmer, by the storms, so, when these repeated gusts of criticism shall have passed away, as we believe ere long they shall, the Scriptures will, no doubt, appear to be more than ever the "word of God which liveth and abideth forever."

In Holland and Germany advanced criticism has during the past twenty-five years had many advocates. In 1886, Kuenen, of Leyden, wrote: "I am no longer advocating a heresy, but am expounding the received view of European critical scholarship." Professor Curtiss, in an article written some years ago, expresses the conclusion that "Lachmann, so far as we know, is the only Old Testament professor in a German university who still defends the Mosaic authorship of the Pentateuch." He might have added that König of Leipzig still held the conservative views on this point.

About the year 1880, Professor Robertson Smith, of Aberdeen, imported some of the German rationalistic methods of criticism into Scotland, and tried the impossible task of pursuing these methods in dealing with the Scriptures, and at the same time of maintaining their distinctively supernatural origin, and their plenary inspiration.

Since that time one and another scholar in Britain and America has drawn, directly or indirectly, on the resources of Germany, and by that means we have, during the last ten years, been made more or less familiar with the term Higher Criticism. Indeed, it has almost become the fashion in some quarters to profess to be a higher critic; and to make this profession is boldly claimed by some to be the only passport which admits its happy possessor to this select circle of really enlightened biblical scholarship. But fashions have their little day, and often change. Those who have not, or do not care to possess, this passport are set aside with a wave of the hand, and their critical opinions go for nothing with the aristocratic biblical scholars. We had always inclined to the opinion that humility and sobriety of mind were essential traits of the true scholar, but the presumption and rashness of many of these modern enlightened critics has greatly perplexed us in continuing to hold this opinion.

In Britain, at the present day, men like Professor Bruce, of Glasgow, Professors Driver and Cheyne, of Oxford, and others, are all more or less in sympathy with advanced critical conclusions regarding the Old Testament Scriptures and the religion of Israel, though Bruce is by no means prepared to go as far as Driver and Cheyne in this direction. In this country, Professors Briggs, Smith, Toy, and others represent the same school of criticism. These scholars boldly claim that their destructive or reconstructive conclusions must prevail. Sometimes, with a coolness that would be amusing, were it not so serious, the conclusions of advanced criticism are assumed to be already fully proved, and schemes of Apologetics or systems of Theology are drawn up under that assumption. We do not venture a prediction here, but we are prompted to ask a question and leave time to give the answer: If the foundations upon which the critics are reconstructing Apologetics and Theology be destroyed, what will the *critics* do?

Then, too, these critics are busy writing books and circulating magazines to advocate their views. To a certain extent they have the ear of many readers, and there are features of attractiveness about their writings. It is possible that the perusal of their writings may be perplexing some honest minds, and threatening to shake their confidence in the Scriptures. Perhaps, also, the foes of Christianity may find in the results of the critics' work, some weapons made ready to their hands for a fresh attack upon the Christian system.

Taking all these things into account, we are inclined to think that every earnest defender of Christianity is bound to examine the methods and conclusions of the critics "to see whether the things which they affirm are so." At the same time, the utmost care should be taken, while rejecting what is false in these methods and conclusions, that we retain firmly in our possession the sound method of dealing with the main questions belonging to that branch of sacred learning which is called Higher Criticism. Above all, if the bold claims of the critics are true, and if it be so that we must abandon our long cherished views, it is only fair that we should know it without delay. But if, as we are convinced will be the case, their methods and conclusions can be shown to be without solid foundation, the sooner this also is understood, the better. In this little book we hope to add at least a mite, as our contribution, to show some weak points in that foundation, and so help some of our readers to understand the ground upon which a refusal to join the ranks of the radical critics may be securely founded.

CHAPTER II.

HIGHER CRITICISM DEFINED.

IN the first chapter we alluded to some introductory matters, and emphasized the serious nature of some of the results, which certain schools of modern criticism are almost forcing upon biblical scholarship at the present day. Our main purpose in that opening chapter was to signalize our firm conviction that the principles and methods of the critics alluded to, are pregnant with serious dangers to the very foundations of the Christian system. Some of the assumptions made, touch the very bases of our religious faith, and the conclusions reached are often startling in their nature. It is not merely important historical and literary questions that are involved in the views of the advanced critics, but in many cases the philosophy of the origin and growth of religion itself is up for discussion. And we feel bound to add that, even if we were convinced that this bold and sometimes arrogant school of criticism is destined to speedy decline and to a premature old age, those who cannot join their ranks or unite with them in their verdicts, should not remain silent, lest by their silence they leave the impression on some minds that the old views of the Bible, and perhaps the Bible itself, are no longer capable of defense. It is under this firm conviction that this little book is written for the wide circle of readers into whose hands it may come.

In this chapter a brief attempt will be made to define the Higher Criticism, and to point out its legitimate function, and thus prepare the way to describe in a general manner those radical forms of it, which have at the present day monopolized the term almost entirely.

The general subject involved belongs to that wide and interesting field of sacred learning known as Biblical Introduction. Biblical Criticism, as a whole, belongs to that field, and may be described as that branch of historical and literary criticism which deals with the various treatises which make up the sacred Scriptures viewed merely as literary and historical productions. It naturally divides itself into two great branches, according to the subject matter which is considered. These are usually termed Lower or Textual Criticism, and Higher or Historical Criticism. It is not easy to assign any good reason why the terms Lower and Higher came to be used as they now are, and it is to be remembered that scholars are not yet agreed as to their proper use, for some writers are disposed to make the internal evidences of the divine origin of the Scriptures the sphere of Lower Criticism, and the external evidences the field for the Higher Criticism. We have simply to use them as we find them, insisting, however, that in no real sense is the one of less value than the other. A brief explanation of each of these great branches of criticism may enable us to mark out more clearly the topics of which we wish specially to treat.

First: Textual Criticism is that branch of the science of biblical criticism which investigates and seeks to determine the exact original text of the various writings of which* the Holy Scriptures are composed. The task of the lower critic is to settle as definitely as possible what the exact language was which the authors of the various books at first wrote down. He seeks to ascertain the text of the autographs of Holy Writ. In doing this the various manuscripts of the Scriptures are collected, collated, and carefully compared. The age of these manuscripts, the form of the letters used, the nature of the vellum upon which they are written, and many other things of minute detail are taken into account by the textual critic in the discharge of his difficult but important office.

Textual Criticism also inspects with care the several versions and translations of the Scriptures, and diligently compares these with the original text, for the purposes of correction, or confirmation. It also estimates the value of the numerous quotations of Scripture found in early and later religious writings, in order thereby to obtain additional information as to what was the precise text of the original manuscripts. In this department of the work, much patient and painstaking work has been done, especially for the New Testament, by scholars like Scholz, Griesbach, Lachmann, Tischendorf, Tregelles, Westcott, and many others. Perhaps the main task which yet remains for the textual critic to perform in biblical study, is to do for the text of the Old Testament what these scholars have done for that of the New.

Secondly: Higher Criticism usually takes for granted the general results of Textual Criticism, and proceeds to investigate various questions as to the origin, date of composition, authorship, and mode of production, of the several writings. In the main, though not exclusively, it is concerned with questions of the authenticity and genuineness of the different books of Scripture, but it at the same time usually emphasizes the inquiry into the mode, or manner, of the composition, or compilation, of these books. The general nature of the books is investigated, and their date, authorship, and value decided on, partly by literary, partly by historical, and partly by subjective tests. The validity of the traditional views, as they are called, is, by certain critics, called in question, and a good deal of freedom is exhibited and frequent hypotheses are announced in regard to the many questions which arise for discussion in this wide and ever-widening field.

In addition, the higher critic inquires particularly into the various sources from which the authors of the sacred writings obtained the materials for their literary productions, and he investigates with almost microscopic care, and sometimes with the personal, or subjective factor largely present, the manifold features of literary idiom and style of the various writings in the Bible. He also extends the scope of his inquiries, and scrutinizes the history and religious institutions of the different peoples alluded to in the Scripture narratives. The literary environment of the biblical authors is thus studied with care, and the higher critic finds himself engaged with a great variety of questions in history, philosophy, ethnology, and comparative religion. His field is wide, his task weighty, so "he should be clothed with humility."

The task, then, which the higher critic undertakes is to answer such questions as these : Are the sacred writings so well attested that we can rely on the statements made therein ? Were the authors candid and trustworthy men, well informed in regard to the matters of which they wrote ? And how is the fact of their inspiration to be viewed in this connection ? Were the real authors the persons whose names stand now connected with the various books ? What was the actual manner of the composition of the writings in question? What were the dates, places, and circumstances of the production of the several books ? Was the work of the reputed authors original composition, compilation of existing documents, or the mere editing of already extant literary materials? Did the development of the religious history of Israel take place in the manner described in the traditional view of the sacred history, or must reconstruction be made in order to get the true view? What view are we to take of the relations between prophecy, ritual, and legislation, as exhibited in the Old Testament, and what view ought we to take of early Christianity as set forth in the New? And what is the precise relation of the ethical monotheism of Israel, in its origin and growth, to the idolatry or polytheism of surrounding nations?

Now any writer who deals with these questions from any point of view may be termed a "higher critic." In a general sense, therefore, he is a higher critic who deals with the questions above stated, and similar questions which lie beyond rather than in the sacred text. That this is a legitimate field for sacred scholarship none should deny. By means of this branch of criticism reverently pursued, much of great value has been furnished to aid in confirming and interpreting the Scriptures.

We wish at this point to emphasize the fact that we shall not allow one school of criticism—the advanced—to drive another—the conservative—off this inviting and fruitful field. The advanced critic cannot claim the field as all his own, till he has won it, and the conservative should never resign the right to deal with these questions till he is fairly driven from the field. He is to be a higher critic, and should not be ashamed of his task nor afraid to do his duty in its performance. But special description of advanced higher criticism must be reserved for our next chapter.

CHAPTER III.

RADICAL HIGHER CRITICISM DEFINED.

IN the last article an attempt was made to define in a general way Lower and Higher Criticism, respectively, and to indicate the topics with which each is specially concerned. With some care the field of Higher Criticism was outlined, and the various questions which it discusses were enumerated. It was also insisted that this is an important and useful department of sacred learning if rightly conducted. At the outset of this article the claim is repeated that the conservative critic has a perfect right to this field, and that he should not be frightened away from it by any of the high and sometimes boastful claims, which the advanced critics make for peculiar critical insight, and profound scholarship.

Nor should the conservative critic be at all irritated, much less discouraged or dismayed, if he be informed, as he sometimes may be, that he is really behind the times, and scarcely qualified to express an opinion that is worth anything upon the questions raised by the Higher Criticism. He need not be disturbed in any measure, if he is set down as a traditionalist; for he may console himself with the reflection, that in quick succession many of the theories of advanced criticism have already become traditional, and others are in danger of speedily suffering the same hard fate.

The conservative critic, therefore, has a duty to do and a legitimate service to render in this connection. He is to deal with all the topics of sacred learning, which properly belong to the field of Higher Criticism. In a reverent, patient, scholarly spirit, he owes it to the cause of truth, and to Him who is the Truth, to handle in the most thorough manner, and according to the methods which are legitimate, even though they be not new, the whole subject matter of which Higher Criticism treats. As between the conservative and advanced critic, it is not simply a question as to which has a right to the field, but rather a question as to which has the best methods, and sets forth the more fully the truth concerning the questions raised. In any case the conservative critic is to be a higher critic as well as a lower, and serve the cause of truth in both fields by pursuing strictly scientific methods of investigation. It should be added that in various ways Lower and Higher Criticism overlap each other.

In this chapter we wish specially to describe what is now known as a particular school of Higher Criticism. Recent critical controversies have to a certain extent narrowed the application of the term Higher Criticism, and in various ways modified its proper meaning. In the popular mind, at least, this is the case to a considerable extent. Not a few intelligent people have the impression that the whole subject of Higher Criticism is a new discovery for which we are indebted to certain biblical scholars in recent times. Some seem inclined to think that the Scriptures were never understood before, and that modern criticism has actually given back Christ to Theology. Others, alarmed at, or disgusted with, the radical results of rationalistic criticism, have too hastily concluded that the whole thing is inherently evil, and ought to be avoided by all devout scholars, but the safe middle view is to hold that there is a reverent and an irreverent, a legitimate and an illegitimate, method of pursuing investigations and reaching conclusions in the field of Higher Criticism. It is the latter which we are now to describe.

It is no easy matter to describe this type of criticism even in a general way. It has received certain new titles, and is known by a variety of names. It is sometimes known as the "newer criticism." Under this title, Dr. Watts, of Belfast, reviewed it at length. Then it is called "advanced criticism," inasmuch as its methods are new and sometimes radical. At times it is described as "historical criticism" in the technical sense, since it professes to follow historical development closely. Again, in some quarters, it is properly described as "rationalistic criticism," inasmuch as it either ignores or denies the supernatural factor in the Scriptures and in the religious system which they unfold. The terms "radical" and "reconstructive" have been applied to it with some propriety, since it touches the basis of the Christian system, and proposes its reconstruction.

Perhaps if the critics of this particular school were allowed to describe themselves, they would say that they represent the critical or historico-critical school of Higher Criticism. A great host of writers in Holland and Germany, with a number in Britain and America, representing almost every shade of opinion from cold rationalism to warm evangelicalism, might be named here. But we defer doing so till we sketch the history of this school of criticism in subsequent articles.

The peculiarity, therefore, about this school of criticism consists not so much in handling the topics which belong to Higher Criticism, as in dealing with them in a particular manner, and under certain presuppositions. It is not the *subject matter* with which it deals, but its *critical method* which distinguishes this school of criticism. It is, in some cases, its general *attitude* toward the questions in hand more than anything else that gives it its peculiar character. In other cases, it is what may be called its *standpoint* in relation to certain fundamental questions which underlie all criticism of the sacred Scriptures, that marks off this school of criticism from others.

Nor is it a question of scholarship merely, nor of mental insight and critical judgment simply, which constitutes the peculiar feature of the school of critics now under our notice. At times we are reminded by its adherents that these qualities are the special heritage of this school, and so it is necessary to point out very clearly that it is not so much their scholarly furnishing for the work of criticism, as the freedom with which the work is done by them that differentiates these particular critics and their work from conservative critics. Not infrequently it is the *spirit* of the critic and his general tone which give him his place in the select circle of higher critics properly so called. From all this we gather that the school of criticism under consideration is marked by its method, attitude, standpoint, and spirit in relation to the general subject matter which belongs to Higher Criticism.

This, of course, is an exceedingly meager description of the modern school of Higher Criticism of which we hear so much at the present day, but it is not possible to speak of it more definitely at this stage without anticipating what can be better stated later on in the course of this treatise, when its history and exposition are to be presented.

Then, too, the difficulty of general description is all the greater on account of the vast variety of opinion existing among the adherents of this particular school. There are reverent critics who profess to hold by the supernatural, and to believe in inspiration, and who are in sympathy with the standpoint and methods of the advanced critical positions. Then there are those who may be termed "evangelical critics," who hold firmly to the simplicity of the gospel as they conceive it, and yet co-operate with this school in its critical campaign. Finally, we have the rationalistic class in this school, who minimize or explain away the supernatural altogether, who take very low views of inspiration, and who are prepared to deal with the sacred Scriptures as if they were in no respect different from any other literature. Some of the rationalistic critics openly set aside the supernatural entirely, and deal with everything on a purely naturalistic plane. It becomes a very important question as to how far the critical views of this whole school can be adopted, and thorough-going rationalistic conclusions be avoided. This question will come up later on in these discussions.

Amid such variety of view, it is not easy to describe in a satisfactory way the particular school of criticism about which we now write. In closing this article we would especially emphasize the fact that it is the *principles* and *methods* of this critical school, which give it its distinctive character. If these principles and methods be essentially rationalistic in their nature, the evangelical and conservative critics are surely warned that they are in doubtful company, and on dangerous ground when they join the ranks of the radical critics. But this must suffice for description, and in the next chapter we shall begin to give some account of the rise and history of this school of criticism.

PART II.

HISTORY OF THE CRITICAL MOVEMENT.

CHAPTER I.

ITS HISTORY.

IN the last chapter a brief and general description of radical Higher Criticism was given. It was particularly pointed out that this school of criticism is distinguished chiefly by its methods, spirit, and general attitude in dealing with the topics it discusses. It was not admitted that this particular school of criticism has any peculiar claim to the field wherein its questions lie. And it is again insisted on that the controversy is not for the *possession* of the field, but in regard to the principles, methods, and results of criticism in that field.

This chapter proposes to begin a brief historical sketch of that critical movement which in various ways has led on to the development of the modern advanced types of Higher Criticism. Such a sketch may have a degree of interest in itself, and it may go far to show how it comes to pass that unsound principles slowly but surely work out disastrous results. And further, we venture to think that a plain outline of the history of the movement will form a valuable critique of the true nature of that school of criticism which is so popular in certain quarters to-day. If the tree be good, we may expect good fruit, but if the tree be corrupt, then we can look only for evil fruit. The historical sketch now to be given may enable us to know the tree by its fruits, or from the fruits to judge the tree.

In the early Christian Church, but little was done in the way of careful criticism or diligent exegetical study of the Scriptures. Men seemed ready to take the plain, simple meaning of the sacred writings, and raise no subtle questions regarding them. Almost the only writer in Patristic times who touched upon the literary and historical questions arising from a critical study of the Scriptures in accordance with rationalistic methods, was Porphyry, who was, let it be carefully noted, one of the chief opponents of Christianity during the latter part of the third century after Christ.

In his opposition to Christianity he sought to point out what he thought were inconsistencies and inaccuracies in the sacred records of the Christian system. In doing so, he examined critically the history of the people of Israel, and made inquiry concerning the origin and development of the Mosaic system. He attacked, at length, the book of Daniel, called in question its date and authorship, sets forth in an exaggerated way certain difficulties in regard to the mode in which the Hebrew Scriptures were composed. In Porphyry, we have, without the pale of the Church, and opposed to Christianity, an acute and learned man, giving hints of those critical principles and methods, which, in modern times, have developed into a well-defined movement within the Christian Church, and among those who are supposed to be the trusted defenders of Christianity. Perhaps the ancient critic was more consistent in making his attack from without, than the modern rationalistic critic is in doing damage from within.

In the latter part of the seventeenth century, we find Spinoza, a celebrated speculative philosopher of the Jewish race, and the father of modern pantheism, entering upon some curious, if not profound, critical enquiries in regard to the Scriptures. In general, he called in question the traditional date and Mosaic authorship of the Pentateuch. He also raised the question whether the complete Mosaic law and ritual as a definite system were historically prior to the development of the Jewish Church and nation in Canaan after the conquest. He did not so much assert that mature Mosaism appeared in the later stages of the Jewish history as cast doubt and uncertainity upon the generally received view among both Jews and Christians of his day.

In his treatise, published in 1670— "*Tractatus Theologico Politicus*"— Spinoza was really the first to ascribe the possible origin of the Pentateuch in its present form to the time of Ezra, if not to Ezra himself. He suggests that the final re-casting of the books, usually regarded as the work of Moses almost entirely, was done by Ezra, and those associated with him. This places these books in their completed form in post-exilic, rather than in pre-exilic times. Spinoza further thinks it likely that Ezra wrote the book of Deuteronomy first, and then afterward composed the remaining books of the Pentateuch. From the examination of the Jewish history and Mosaic ritual which he makes, he thinks the reasonable conclusion to be that the definite and complete religious system of the Jewish people belongs to a much later age than the time of Moses, of Joshua, and of the conquest of Canaan.

There is much about the philosophy and critical views of Spinoza that is of the deepest interest and importance. He was a Jew, who, for some not very clearly understood reason, was excommunicated. He is described as a gentle, devout man, who found his chief delight in the realms of speculative philosophy. Still, it is barely possible that he was prompted to criticise the history and religion of his own people by the irritation which he must have felt toward those who put him out of the synagogue. This possibility, we are inclined to think, should be kept in mind in estimating the critical views of this acute Jew.

Spinoza was a pantheist. He identified the universal substance, or ground of all existence, with the Divine Being. This universal "substance" or being has for man's apprehension two attributes,—extension and thought. All finite existences are modes of these attributes. These modifications take place in such a purely necessary way that everything is either natural, or supernatural, according as we please to use the terms. In religion, the development must take place in the same necessitarian way, and the distinction between the natural and the supernatural operations of Deity is thereby obliterated. Now, it is worth while observing here, and we allude to Spinoza's pantheism specially for this purpose, the somewhat remarkable fact that the first great exponent of modern pantheism is also the virtual author of the radical, or rationalistic theory of the religion and ritual of Israel, which has, in recent years, caused so much controversy among biblical scholars. This fact will appear all the more striking when we see, as we shall later on in this sketch, that modern idealistic pantheism, and radical views of the questions in Higher Criticism, emerge side by side in Germany. We naturally wonder whether there is any logical and natural connection between these two things.

Soon after Spinoza, though in many respects opposed to him, we find Richard Simon, about the year 1678, dealing with some of these critical questions. He quite openly discarded his belief in the unity of the Pentateuch and in its Mosaic authorship. At the same time he allowed that there may have been some kind of legislative kernel of the law which came from Moses. Mature Mosaism, however, he distinctly held, was a development only found complete from the days of Ezra onward. Simon gives us thus more definite views than Spinoza suggested.

A few years later, in 1685, Clericus unfolded views which were even more radical and startling than those of Simon. In substance he maintained that the Pentateuch and Mosaism belong to a much later date than the Exodus from Egypt; and he was bold enough to venture the assertion that it owed its origin to some Jewish priest who lived soon after the overthrow of the ten tribes, and perhaps about the year 588 B. C. With these writers the movement seems to have exhausted itself for the time being, and so for over a century we hear little about these new theories of the Old Testament history.

At this point we may properly close this article. Already we have seen that the essential elements of rationalistic critical theory originated outside of, and in opposition to, the Church. We cannot fail to note the fact, also, that the modern critic's claim for originality is seriously impaired by what Simon and Clericus presented two centuries ago.

CHAPTER II.

ITS HISTORY CONTINUED.

IN our last chapter the history of advanced or rationalistic Higher Criticism was commenced. The opinions of Porphyry, Spinoza, Simon, and Clericus were briefly sketched. The important place of Spinoza, the father of modern pantheism, in originating some of the radical theories of modern criticism, was signalized, and the striking connection between pantheism and negative criticism was pointed out. In this article we continue the historical sketch we have in view.

Our last chapter closed with the end of the seventeenth century, and at that period speculation upon the critical problems presented by the sacred Scriptures subsided for a time. During the eighteenth century these critical theories of the Old Testament literature and religion, together with the pantheism of Spinoza, were generally rejected. Only here and there do we find any favorable allusion to them, and then usually by the opponents of Christianity as a supernatural religion.

The attacks made upon the Christian faith during this century were philosophical rather than critical in their nature. These attacks are represented by deism in England, materialism in France, and rationalism in Germany. Almost the only writer among the English deists who raised questions of a critical or literary nature regarding the Scriptures, was Collins, who wrote about the beginning of the eighteenth century. Collins examined prophecy, and sought to show that Christianity is founded on various misinterpretations of Jewish prophecy into which our Lord and his apostles unconsciously blundered. His work is by no means profound, and yet it is of some historic interest in this sketch, for it further illustrates the critical movement as still outside the Church, and against Christianity. In Germany the beginning of the rationalistic movement belongs to the close of the eighteenth century, as we shall see a little later on in our sketch.

At this stage in the history of rationalistic critical speculation, it is proper to give some account of the influence of a writer whose character and work are often little understood. We refer to Jean Astruc, a celebrated physician, first at Toulouse, and afterward for many years at Paris, in France. He was the son of a Protestant pastor, who recanted at the revocation of the Edict of Nantes, and entered the Romish Church, but virtually renounced religion altogether, for he became a lawyer, and lived as a philosopher. Jean Astruc was born in 1684, and was professor in the medical school at Toulouse from 1710 to 1729. In the latter year, with wealth and wide reputation for medical knowledge, he removed to Paris, where he lived till 1766. He was professor in the College Royal, had extensive practice as a physician, and moved in what was then regarded as the best social circles in the gay French capital.

It is worth while noting further the fact that he was on intimate terms in Paris with the free thinkers of that unbelieving age. Here he was often one of that literary circle which embraced men like Fontenelle, Montesquieu, Voltaire, Bolingbroke, Chesterfield, and other kindred spirits, whose disregard for Christianity is well known. There is good reason to believe that his private life for nearly twenty years was not without serious blemish. He became intimate soon after he came to Paris with the notorious Madame de Tencin, whose whole life was a succession of intrigue, vice, and crime. At her death he succeeded in getting possession of over 200,000 francs of her property. Little more need be said of the character of Astruc, and we conclude our allusion to it by an expression from Voltaire, and one from Grimm Voltaire describes him as "miser, debauchee, and possessed with a devil." Grimm says, "Astruc was one of the men most decried in Paris. He was regarded as a rascal, a cheat, vicious—in a word, as a very dishonest man." Such is the man who originated the "documentary hypothesis," of which modern criticism has made so much.

In 1753 Astruc published his work entitled,

"Conjectures concerning the Original Memoranda, which it appears Moses used to Compose the Book of Genesis, with Remarks which Support or Throw Light on these Conjectures." This treatise is now a very rare one, for the reason that when the French Parliament was about to make inquiry concerning it, Astruc bought up and burned every copy he could purchase or procure. It was issued in Paris, and yet by its title page it professed to have been published in Brussels, so, as a matter of fact, it was sent forth with a falsehood on its face. Why it was written by a man in Astruc's position it is hard to understand. He professes a desire to remove difficulties from the sacred Scriptures, and yet his work played at once into the hands of unbelief. Against this we are not aware that Astruc ever made the slightest protest.

In his *Conjectures*, he points out the use of the two names applied to God in Genesis, Jehovah and Elohim, and alludes to what he thinks needless repetitions, anachronisms, and interpolations, together with the general disorder in many of the narratives in this book. He accounts for these things by supposing that Moses was merely the human compiler of the treatise, and unconsciously blundered in his work. In this way Moses may have been honest, but he was evidently ignorant, and his narratives can scarcely be trustworthy, much less inspired.

In working out his theory, Astruc placed the text of Genesis in three main columns, which he marked A, B, and C. Then various fragments, as he thought, of the literature, which could not be fitted into these three sections, he placed in ten additional columns. The original memoranda, Astruc supposes, came partly from the Jews and partly from other nations. Moses, he assumes, just put these together, leaving all their agreements and differences just as he found them. Professing to remove difficulties, it is evident that Astruc multiplied them a thousandfold. Voltaire even, in a review of Astruc's work, says of it, with fine and pointed irony, that "it redoubles the darkness he sought to disperse."

We have thus dwelt upon the author and origin of the famous "documentary hypothesis," in such a way as to set both in the clear light of history, and to show that it was invented by a bad man, not really in the interests of Christianity, or biblical scholarship, but indirectly at least to supply weapons against the divine origin of the Scriptures of the Christian system. We also set forth these things concerning the origin of the documentary hypothesis in order to put immature scholars and youthful biblical students on their guard in reference to the admissions which are often made concerning the "documentary hypothesis." For ourselves we do not like its birth-place, and we cannot grow fond of its company.

We have already stated that these radical theories did not appear on German soil till about the end of the last century. When the idealistic pantheism of Schelling and Hegel was popularized by Lessing and Goethe, and so made more accessible for the common people both in prose and verse, about the close of the last century and the opening of this, we find these speculations again making their appearance. At first, here and there, in a timid or cautious way, attempts were made to reproduce the post-exilian theory of the origin of the ritual, legislation, and literature of the religion of Israel. These radical opinions began to crystallize into definite form early in the present century, and in the hands of professedly Christian scholars. It was at this point that these theories succeeded in scaling the walls of the citadel of Christianity; or rather it was at this time that some of the unwise occupants of the citadel, who should have been its defenders, opened the gates to let these radical anti-supernaturalistic speculations come within the walls.

In our next chapter we shall proceed to give some account of what they did when they were inside.

CHAPTER III.

ITS HISTORY CONTINUED.

IN our last chapter the history of advanced or rationalistic criticism was continued. The greater part of the chapter was taken up with a brief account of Astruc, the originator of the "documentary hypothesis." In Astruc we still have the critical speculation without the Church. At the close of the chapter, it was indicated that just about the beginning of the present century, the gates were opened to allow these theories of advanced criticism to enter the Church. This brings us to Germany, and calls upon us to give some account of that great critical and rationalistic movement which, in varying forms, has continued down to the present time.

In the year 1806, De Wette published a treatise on a part of the Old Testament, and in 1817 he issued a work of a critical and historical nature on the whole Old Testament Scriptures. In these two works he set forth the view that we must look to the time of Josiah for the book of Deuteronomy, and that the history set forth in the sacred books must be reconstructed in order to get at the true state of the case. He broke up the Pentateuch into a series of parts, differing in age, origin, and contents, and expressed the opinion that the Levitical ritual came into existence at a late stage in the history of the religious life of the people. He also denies the Davidic origin and Messianic nature of many of the Psalms, and although he does not give a naturalistic explanation of the miracles, he is inclined to favor the legendary nature of the narratives concerning the miracles of the Old Testament. Here we find the favorite theory of certain modern schools of criticism in its main outlines advocated by De Wette, who was largely dominated, though not entirely controlled, by the thoroughly rationalistic methods and spirit of Paulus.

Some time later, about the year 1830, two writers, both of them exponents of the philosophy of Hegel, presented even more radical and thoroughgoing views. Their names are Vatke and Leopold George. They asserted without reserve that the whole Mosaic ritual and legislation contained in the Pentateuch was post-Mosaic, and the greater part of it, also, post-prophetic. They further held that Deuteronomy was written about the time of the Exile, and that it is the oldest, not the latest book of the Mosaic law. The other four books, Genesis, Exodus, Leviticus, and Numbers, were written after Deuteronomy, and so subsequently to the Exile. These books, they further asserted, were to be regarded as almost entirely mythical in their nature.

Vatke was one of the early writers who developed what came in later times to be known as the "Wellhausen Theory" of the Old Testament. He expressly maintained that the mature ritual and sacrificial system of the Pentateuch was post-exilic, and his mythical ideas of the Old Testament were the precursors of Strauss's mythical explanation of the New Testament narratives. Throughout we clearly see the rationalistic spirit and attitude in those scholars within the Church who first gave expression to those radical theories now under review.

In the year 1833 we come to an important era in the progress of advanced critical speculation. In that year Edward Reuss, of Strasbourg, published a treatise in which the critical theory was presented in a much more elaborated form. He reproduced the main points in Spinoza's Ezra hypothesis, and followed up the speculations of De Wette and Vatke. In this way he gave much more definite outline to the theory of the later origin of the ritual, legislation, and literature involved in the religion of Israel. In Reuss we have, indeed, the distinct commencement of those definite theories, which, in quite recent times, have developed into the main positions maintained by advanced, or radical, Higher Criticism on the Old Testament field. The work of Reuss is full of interest on this account. He also claims to have really preceded Vatke and George in reaching his conclusions, so that it is not easy to decide to whom the honor of priority really belongs. He gives prominence to the historical side of his critical work, and he opposed with vigor and success, in later years, the views of the Tübingen school.

By the year 1848 we find these general critical views adopted by many scholars in Germany. It would seem that by degrees, during the period from 1833 to 1848, the Mosaic authorship of the Pentateuch and the early rise in the days of the Exodus of mature Mosaism, were rejected by the majority of critics. Only a few here and there held consistently by the old orthodox view, and the Scripture narratives of both Old and New Testaments were handled with a freedom that paid scanty regard to their divine origin and inspiration.

The older rationalism, which rested largely on the deistic philosophy of the relation of God to his works, gradually gave place to the idealistic pantheism of the Hegelian philosophy. The result of this was that in the field of biblical criticism we do not hear so much of the naturalistic attempts to explain the miracles and other phases of the supernatural. We find the effort now to be rather in the direction of harmonizing the Scripture narratives with, or reconstructing them if necessary, according to, the essential principles of the idealistic evolution of the system of Hegel. According to this system, as with every phase of pantheism, everything must be regarded as either natural or supernatural; consequently the distinction between the two is virtually obliterated. This being done, the entire Scripture narratives, with the system of religion they set forth, must be explained in accordance with this philosophical standpoint. If the contents of the narratives, as they stand, do not agree with the order thus rendered necessary, reconstruction must be made, and from this standpoint the critic enters on his task. Up to this point we have seen some of the results in the case of the Old Testament.

It soon became evident, however, that a similar mode of criticism might be applied to the Gospel narratives which set forth the life of Christ. It was very natural to conclude that if the critical procedure in the case of the Old Testament led to a rejection of the so-called traditional views regarding it, the next logical step to take was to apply the same methods to Christ and the New Testament narratives. Accordingly, in the year 1835, just about the time that Vatke and Reuss revived Spinoza's Ezra hypothesis, and suggested the mythical origin of large parts of the first four books of Moses, we find that Strauss published his "Leben Jesu." This "Life of Christ" is in many respects a bold and remarkable book, and its appearance produced an immense sensation in the world of theological learning. It soon called forth vigorous replies from both the dogmatic and historical standpoints. Among the best of these are Dorner's "Person of Christ," and Neander's "Life of Christ." Later writers have dealt with the theory of Strauss at length, and effectively exploded the whole speculation. Christlieb's critique of Strauss is also very fine.

No attempt need be made here to expound and criticise the mythical hypothesis which Strauss set forth to explain the Gospel narratives. It is virtually an application of Vatke's mythical views of the Old Testament to the Gospel history of the New. On the philosophical side, Strauss is allied with the idealistic pantheism of Hegel, whose disciple the great destructive critic of the New Testament was. This theory does not exert much influence at the present day, nor has it many adherents, still in current literature we sometimes see the spirit of the mythical theory floating about. Moreover, we see in the absurd and unhistorical nature of this theory how far unsound modes of Higher Criticism will lead, if once we are committed to them. The theory itself may be a mummy neatly embalmed, but its ghost, we fear, still lives. At this point this chapter must close.

CHAPTER IV.

ITS HISTORY CONTINUED.

THE preceding chapter continued the history of the radical movement of Higher Criticism. The views and theories of De Wette, Vatke, George, and Reuss in the Old Testament, and of Strauss in the New Testament field were briefly sketched. During the period of about thirty years in which these writers set forth their theories, the tendency was toward a purely rational explanation of the religion and literature of the sacred Scriptures. In this tendency the mythical feature was a very prominent one in the hands of Vatke for the Old Testament, and Strauss for the New. Above all, we cannot fail to notice that these reconstructive theories usually went hand in hand with a denial of the supernatural element in the Scriptures.

This chapter continues the history, and will bring it forward to the present generation. In the year 1847 another important stage was reached in the development of these critical theories. In that year F. C. Baur, of Tübingen, published a treatise in which he elaborated some peculiar critical views which soon came to be known as those of the Tübingen school. Baur was a Hegelian in philosophy, and applied the dialectic of that philosophy to explain, in a purely natural way, the New Testament and the beginning of Christianity. The result was the production of the "Tendency Theory," which is really based on Hegel's "Philosophy of History."

According to the "Tendency Theory" advocated by Baur, there were several distinct tendencies of doctrinal view in the New Testament times. Two at least are prominent, and a third may be observed. The two chief tendencies are the Pauline and the Petrine, while the Johannine is not so distinct. By the application of Hegel's logical principles to these supposed early natural tendencies, the antithesis between them was resolved in a higher synthesis by which, in a purely natural way, the divergent views were harmonized. The result was an onward step in the growth of the Christian system in its early stages.

Later on in the Ebionitic and Gnostic heresies we have, as Baur thinks, renewed antitheses which again are to be resolved in another and a higher synthesis. In this way, by a mediating process of a logical nature, the successive antitheses were resolved in successive syntheses, and in the end, about the beginning of the third century, catholic or complete Christianity was the result. In this way the facts of history are made to fit the logical conditions of a peculiar and subtle philosophical theory. The supernatural is eliminated, and the most we can say concerning early Christianity is that it was the product of a kind of transcendental logic working in the religious history of the apostolic age.

Then in harmony with this theory of the origin of the religion of New Testament times the production of the different books of Scripture is accounted for. Each book, whether Gospel narrative or doctrinal epistle, was written to support one or other of these "tendencies," or to mediate between opposing tendencies. Much diversity of view exists among the advocates of this theory in regard to the authorship and date of the several books. In general, the Gospels are supposed to have been written from 130 to 170 A. D., and the Epistles are arranged in a most arbitrary way, as Pauline, Petrine, and Mediative, as the case may seem to require, according to the judgment of the critic. One would almost suppose that Baur and his associates had been present when Christianity was passing through its early stages, and that they had been looking over the shoulders of the sacred writers as they were penning their narratives.

Our purpose is not to criticise this theory at length. It has fallen entirely into decay; or perhaps it would be better to say that it has gone quite out of fashion, for there seem to be fashions in criticisms as well as in bonnets and coats. Hilgenfeld was for many years, almost the only representative of the tendency theory. Recently, however, Pfleiderer of Berlin has been making some efforts to rehabilitate Baur's theory, and to secure for it a bearing through the *Gifford Lectures* in Scotland.

It is worth while noting the fact that the theories of Strauss and Baur are often classed together, as if they were substantially alike in their essential principles. Strauss and Renan are in much closer affinity than Strauss and Baur. The mythical and legendary are more akin than are the mythical and tendency theories. The root idea in the theory of Strauss, is that of the *mythus* naturally expanding; in the legendary scheme of Renan, it is an accretion gathering about a basis of fact; and in the tendency theory of Baur, it is a necessary logical process bringing forth its historical product in early Christianity and its literature. In the case of the mythical theory, the literature is an unconscious growth; and in that of the tendency scheme, it is an intentional product. With Strauss, the several books mark the form that the *mythus* had reached, while with Baur they were written to support the *tendencies* already existing.

The views of Baur have been vigorously criticised, and successfully refuted by writers on the Continent and in Britain, and they do not meet with much favor at the present day. In this way rationalistic Higher Criticism, within Christianity itself, was compelled to confess failure in another attempt to account for the religion of the New Testament on the basis of pure rationalism. Moreover, this work of refutation greatly confirmed the strictly historical views of the Christ of history. Just as the same blast which lays prostrate the loosely rooted poplar tree only fixes more firmly the roots of the sturdy oak, so the refutation of these baseless theories of Higher Criticism confirms the true historical view of the sacred Scriptures and their religious system.

During the last twenty or thirty years there are several names which must have a place, even in a brief sketch like this. At the same time a host of writers who have supported advanced critical theories cannot have even their names mentioned in the space at our disposal. There are four chief names to be set down as prominent in recent developments in the critical school up to about the year 1880. These are Graf, Kuenen, Wellhausen, and Robertson Smith.

Graf was a pupil of Reuss, the Strasburg critic. In 1860 he propounded what may be called the *negative critical theory* of the Pentateuch, and with him we find advanced rationalistic criticism back on the territory of the Old Testament again. This general theory, usually known as "Graf's Theory," marks a still more definite stage in the progress of critical speculation. Others who followed him gave the theory much more complete and detailed form, still the essential outlines of those critical theories, so popular in certain quarters at the present day, were sketched by Graf.

As this general theory will be stated more fully in subsequent articles, we need not add anything further in the historical statement we are now making than to mention this fact.

The second name above mentioned is that of Kuenen of Leyden. Kuenen is often set down as a German, but he is a Hollander and wrote in Dutch. In 1865 he completed the publication of an extended work of a critical and historical nature concerning the Old Testament, and in 1882 he issued another treatise in which he applied the advanced higher critical methods to the books of Moses and the history of Israel. Kuenen adopted substantially the leading outlines of Graf's theory, and with great wealth of learning and boldness of speculation he expounded it more fully, giving it much more detailed completeness of structure. He denied the reality of the supernatural in the Scriptures, and thereby set aside their inspiration. Kuenen is certainly an able and scholarly writer, from a certain point of view, and in some respects his is the most influential hand that has aided in giving form to the critical theory.

The next writer to be mentioned is Wellhausen, — of Greifswald, till 1882. In 1878 he published his "History of Israel," which has had an extensive circulation. In this treatise he gave the Grafian hypothesis still greater completeness, and presented it in the general form in which it is now current among rationalistic critics. In this complete form it may be known as the Graf-Wellhausen Theory of the history of Israel, and of the literature and religious system found in the Old Testament.

In general this theory maintains that the complete Mosaic ritual and legislation originated after the period of the prophets, and that the Pentateuch in its present form was compiled after the Exile. It is not necessary to enter into details here, as future chapters will give full exposition of this theory.

We reserve what we have to say concerning Robertson Smith, for the next chapter. In this way we will make the transition from Germany to Britain, and find the advanced theories of Historical or Higher Criticism passing from Teutonic to Anglo-Saxon circles. How they have flourished there we shall also see in the next chapter, and with that chapter the history of the radical reconstructive movement will conclude.

CHAPTER V.

ITS HISTORY CONCLUDED.

THE last chapter dealt with the history of rationalistic criticism during a period of about thirty years, from 1847 to 1878. The chief names which appeared during this period, were Baur, Graf, Kuenen, and Wellhausen. Baur's Tendency theory of the New Testament and of the origin of Christianity in a purely natural way was described, and the part which the other three authors played in shaping modern critical theories of the Old Testament was briefly indicated.

At the close of the chapter, allusion was made to Robertson Smith, and to the fact that with him the radical speculations passed from Germany to Britain, and so from Teutonic to Anglo-Saxon circles. At this point we take up the history and hope to complete it in this chapter.

Robertson Smith was formerly a professor in the Free Church College at Aberdeen, Scotland. He early showed aptitude for linguistic studies, and spent some time as a student in Germany at Bonn and Göttingen. After teaching as assistant in physics in Edinburgh University for two years, he became professor of Hebrew in the Free Church

College at Aberdeen in 1870. In 1881 he was removed from his Chair by the Assembly, on account of his heretical teaching upon points involved in the radical critical theories of the Graf-Wellhausen School. In 1883 he went to Cambridge University as professor of Arabic, and since 1886, he has been librarian of that University.[1] Soon after the General Assembly removed him from his Chair at Aberdeen, he became editor of the ninth edition of the Encyclopedia Britannica, and the impress of his views is seen in many of the articles on biblical subjects in this great work. To say the least, many of these articles are one-sided, and by no means do justice to conservative opinions in regard to critical questions. Indeed, some of these articles seem to be written in the interests of radical criticism, and to entirely ignore the conservative views.

Smith's articles in the Britannica, on "The Bible," and on "The Hebrew Literature," first attracted attention. Then his books on "The Prophets of Israel," and on "The Old Testament in the Jewish Church," set forth his views at length, subsequent to his removal from his Chair at Aberdeen, though the lectures contained in the latter book were delivered during the period that his case was before the Assembly. On the ground of the views expressed in the articles above named,

[1] Since this was written, Dr. Smith has died at the early age of forty-nine years.

and in other ways, he was charged with heresy, and after a heated controversy in which he made a vigorous and able defense, he was removed from his Chair.

All that need be said in this historical sketch regarding Smith's writings, is, that there is really little new in them. He has evidently a bright mind, is a brilliant scholar in certain lines, and is master of a splendid style of writing. It cannot be said that his scholarship is either broad, accurate, or well balanced; and in the perusal of his writings the reader is often impressed with the fact that general conclusions are drawn from slender premises, and sweeping inductions made from a few isolated facts. What Smith has done may not unfairly be called a work of importation. He taught German rationalistic criticism how to speak the English tongue. In other words, he has simply put into good English dress the main outlines of the Graf-Wellhausen hypothesis concerning the religion and literature of Israel, slightly modifying the style of the clothes to suit the Anglo-Saxon wearer. At the same time he endeavored to hold by the doctrine of inspiration, while following the methods and adopting the general conclusions of that school of criticism which sets aside the reality of the supernatural and which thereby sweeps overboard all semblance of inspiration in the Scriptures. Perhaps the masters were more consistent than their Scotch pupil, even though the pupil was more reverent than his Teutonic masters. We mention these things chiefly for the benefit of those who think that there is profound originality in the writings of the English-speaking higher critics. We are perhaps not going too far when we say that their main business is importation, rather than production; and, in some cases, if we make close inspection of the stock in trade, we may discover that most of it is second-hand goods. An English-speaking professor, decked out in the well-worn study gown of his German preceptor, is scarcely an edifying spectacle in those circles of biblical scholarship which claim so much originality.

This virtually brings our historical sketch down to our own day, and we conclude it with some brief descriptive allusions to the present situation in regard to the advanced school of criticism. So far as Germany is concerned, little need be said. Judging from statements that have lately come to us from various quarters and which may be relied on, there seems to be a tendency in the fatherland to return to more conservative ground in regard to the literary and critical questions round which the fires of criticism have been burning so fiercely for the past forty years. While there is no decided reaction against the Graf-Wellhausen position, still some of its boldest features are modified in the literature at present coming from that quarter, and several influential critics are in open revolt against the methods of this reigning school of criticism.

After the controversy in Robertson Smith's case subsided, mutterings of coming debate began to be heard on this side of the Atlantic. Indeed, so early as 1879, Professor Toy, of the Southern Baptist Theological Seminary announced opinions in regard to some critical questions which speedily led to his withdrawal from that institution. Since 1880, he has been professor of Hebrew at Harvard University, and in 1884 published a book on "The History of the Religion of Israel," which showed that he was in hearty sympathy with the advanced methods and results of radical criticism, and had, indeed, already drawn from the writings of the Germans to a considerable extent.

A few years later the center of interest was removed to Union Seminary, New York, and all our readers are familiar with the proceedings in the case of Professor Briggs, since the delivery of his Inaugural Address in 1891. For some time before, it had been supposed that Professor Briggs was teaching some advanced views, not unlike those prevalent in Germany and set forth by the Graf-Wellhausen school. During the two years which followed the delivery of his famous address till he was suspended from the ministry of the Presbyterian Church, it became more and more apparent that Professor Briggs was on radical ground. He insisted that he held fast by the inspiration of the sacred Scriptures, but the principles and methods to which he had committed himself made it difficult, if not impossible, for him to hold a consistent doctrine of inspiration in harmony with his critical methods and conclusions.

Recrossing the Atlantic, we find that in recent years, the quiet retreats of scholastic leisure at Oxford, have been invaded by radical opinions in regard to biblical criticism. The two names connected with this invasion are Professors Driver and Cheyne. Driver has been professor of Hebrew since 1882, and Cheyne, professor of Biblical Interpretation since 1885. Various publications soon showed the trend of Driver's views, till his book on "The Introduction to the Literature of the Old Testament," appeared two years ago. In this book he is committed to a modified form of the Wellhausen theory, and a hasty perusal of this treatise shows how extensively Driver has been engaged in the business of importation of critical views from Germany, where the manufacture of theories is carried on so extensively. It would seem that Cheyne was unwilling that his fellow-professor should have all the fame of original critical inventions, and so he has recently published several articles in which he takes even more radical views than Driver, especially in regard to the Psalms.

At present, in Britain many other scholars of lesser note are adopting these views, but our space forbids further description. Suffice it to say that there seems to be a *craze*, almost, in regard to these views, so that in certain quarters it is exceedingly out of the fashion to avow adherence to the conservative position in regard to the literature and religion of the Scriptures, especially of that set forth in the Old Testament. It is a comfort to remember that fashions change frequently.

The last slight breeze in the critical field is associated with the name of President Harper, of Chicago University. He has, it seems, in a course of recent lectures, been stating some advanced views in regard to the early narratives of the Old Testament. Whether this is to be accounted for as a result of the Parliament of Religions, or arises from an unconscious ambition to have Chicago in the van, or springs from the effort of another biblical critic to be original, we are not prepared to say. Perhaps the truth is that Harper has unconsciously gone into the importation business also; and, if we are not greatly mistaken, some of the materials which he has been dressing up for the itching ears of his Chicago auditors may be discovered in the writings of radical or rationalistic critics. It is only fair to add that Harper would not allow us to classify him with the Wellhausen school. He has recently criticised that school, so that we are glad to see signs of a hopeful reaction in his case.

We close this chapter, and with it our historical sketch, with a very brief reference to some names on the conservative side. In Germany, though radical opinions in criticism have had great prominence during the past fifty years, yet the radical critics by no means have had things all their own way. Ranke refuted in a thorough manner that phase of radical theory known as the fragmentary hypothesis, and Kurtz dealt deadly blows against the supplementary form of the hypothesis. Hengstenberg along several lines provides much material for the vindication of the conservative side in the controversy. Hävernick, Drechsler, Bachmann, Kiel, and Delitzsch have all more or less decidedly combatted the radical views. And at the present day König, and especially Klostermann, are making such vigorous attacks upon the Wellhausen theory that unless some one comes speedily to the rescue that critical stronghold will be captured or destroyed. Other names of prominence in Germany on the conservative side might be mentioned did space permit. Professor Watts, of Belfast, has been a strong opponent of the advanced views in Britain, and Professor W. H. Green, of Princeton, has done noble service on the conservative side, in this country. Professors Osgood, Bissell, and Warfield, with a host of others, have, in a thoroughly scholarly way, rebutted the radical views. Professor Robertson, of Glasgow, in his "Early Religion of Israel," has given a book which must be answered by the radicals before they can continue their onward way. The *Presbyterian and Reformed Review* for several years has rendered splendid service in guiding devout scholarship into safe lines, and in leading it to sound conclusions. But we must conclude history and description, and in the next chapter begin our work in the "Exposition of Advanced Criticism."

PART III.

EXPOSITION OF ADVANCED HIGHER CRITICISM.

CHAPTER I.

PRELIMINARY.

WITH the last chapter, the outline of the history of advanced Higher Criticism which our limits permitted us to give, was completed. During the course of the history, at least one striking fact very clearly emerged. Even the brief sketch we were able to give shows that what now claims to be the only sound, scientific, and scholarly school of Higher Criticism within the Christian Church began its career without the Church, and was often used as a weapon against the Christian system. It was born in the world outside the Church, and has only been adopted into the Christian household in modern times. The three great names already mentioned as having much to do with the origin of advanced theories and methods — Porphyry, Spinoza, and Astruc — were all without the Church, and in some cases they were the bitter foes of Christianity.

This is a fact which does not seem always to be fully considered by some reverent critics who have a degree of sympathy with the new methods and principles of advanced criticism. It remains to be seen how this adopted worldling, which some

Christian scholars have brought into the household of faith, will, in the course of time, treat its foster parents. It may be that it will prove itself to be exceedingly unfilial, and do much harm to, even as it has already caused not a little trouble in, the household. We should make sure that the little pagan is not only civilized, but Christianized, before we allow it to have a place within the family circle of Christianity.

Let it be kept constantly in mind, therefore, that the methods and theories advocated by modern Higher Criticism originated on non-Christian soil, were brought into the Church by rationalistic hands during the eighteenth century, and are, perhaps, all the more dangerous now that they are within the sacred inclosure. For those who desire to retain supernatural views of Christianity, it must be an awkward, and perhaps a dangerous thing to attempt to square these critical theories with the supernaturalism implied in the Christian system. This critical speculation may prove a viper which Christianity takes into her bosom, and which in turn may inflict serious injury upon, if it does not endanger the life of, the system.

When continental critics deny the reality of the supernatural in Christianity and set aside the inspiration of the sacred Scriptures, and then proceed, in a consistent way, with their work of destructive criticism, it cannot but be a bold if not a foolhardy venture for British or American critics to pursue the methods and adopt the theories of these critics, and at the same time hope to retain intact the high claims which Christianity makes to be unique and divine. Their aims may be honest and their purpose resolute, yet we are much afraid that the Anglo-Saxon reproducers of Teutonic critical theories will find themselves driven to minimize the supernatural, and perhaps repudiate it altogether.

Let this danger be fully considered by those who feel drawn to these speculations. There is a fascination about them which tends to dazzle the eyes of an inquiring and venturesome mind, but great care should be taken to prevent these novel theories from perverting sound judgment in questions of criticism, which, to a large extent, must always be matters of fact. What is needed is the exercise of sober caution on the part of those who deal with these questions, lest some who are always anxious to hear some new theory may be carried away by baseless though beautiful theories.

It may take several generations to mature among us the serious results which we fear must follow the adoption of these advanced critical views of the literature and religion of the sacred Scriptures. Many things during the last ten years constrain us to believe that the general adoption of the critical theories, now so popular in certain circles, by English-speaking critics and biblical scholars, would, by the inexorable logic of events, open wide the gate for a deluge of rationalism to flow through the

Church, which would make shipwreck of Christianity as a supernatural system of religion.

On the other hand, while we say all this, we wish it to be most distinctly understood that we are not averse to, nor do we in any way oppose or discourage the most thorough and scholarly study of everything connected with the Christian system. We invite the deep thinker to inspect its philosophical foundations; we ask the careful student of nature to make a reverent survey of the broad fields covered by revelation; we welcome the social reformer to make an honest estimate of the principles of Christianity in their bearing on the social welfare of the human race; and we gladly encourage the most careful critical study of the sacred Scriptures of the Christian system by the lower and higher, critics alike. We repeat what has been stated in a former chapter, to the effect that we believe in the reverent study of many of the questions with which Higher Criticism deals. The conservative critic has an especially important work to do in this field at the present day. This service he should seek faithfully to render, even among the Babel of critical tongues to which he may be compelled to listen. With sound principles under his feet, and right methods in his hands, the conservative critic should address himself to the task his age sets before him, and by thorough, scholarly investigation seek to establish correct conclusions, and at the same time explode the false theories which a hasty criticism boldly expounds.

It will thus be evident that our objection is not lodged against Higher Criticism as a branch of biblical study, but against the false principles and unsound methods by which advanced critics are controlled in their investigations. It is against these that we wage war, just as we would resist the false and unsound everywhere. And, in our judgment, the work of the conservative critic is to join in this warfare ; and he should never dream of leaving the field entirely to the liberal school of criticism.

All this naturally leads to another line of remark upon which we desire to say a word or two as preliminary to the "Exposition of Advanced Criticism," upon which we are presently to enter. What we have in view and wish to emphasize, is the great importance, perhaps we might say the urgent necessity, of an acquaintance with recent phases of modern Higher Criticism by the ministry of the Christian Church. The advanced school of criticism in Anglo-Saxon circles is aggressive, and in many respects scholarly. Their writings are abundant, and their circulation is diligently pushed. Magazine and review articles, single treatises, and even International Libraries are used to spread abroad the new critical theories. Moreover, these writings are often quite popular in their style, and thereby secure attention and hearing, when heavier treatises would not be read at all. We cannot shut our eyes to the fact that the literature of this school is widely read, and doubtless many minds, yet immature, are unconsciously affected by it. However we may account for the fact, the truth of the statement just made cannot be denied. Whether it be love of novelty, or the desire to learn the truth, or the literary attractiveness of the style, or the leaning of the natural mind toward opinions which are naturalistic, we may not be able to say. One thing we do know, and that is that the advanced school has secured a hearing in a wide circle, and the radical theories have come forth from the retreats of the scholar. We are thus taught in various ways, and in such forms that intelligent people are now made more or less familiar with some of the main features of these theories. '

In these circumstances it is very necessary that conservative critics should arise and deal with these questions in a plain and attractive manner, and not allow the liberals to carry the palm for thorough scholarship, and for literary finish. We are well aware that the conservatives have not been nor are they now idle ; but the impression seems to be left on some minds that there is room for further thorough-going treatment of the questions from the conservative standpoint. In our humble judgment, the work to be done is to follow the pathway which the advanced critics have traveled, examining their alleged facts as well as testing their proposed theories, in order to exhibit the weakness of the advanced critical position, and in turn to show how the conservative position may be not only sustained, but confirmed by the very latest results of sound biblical scholarship. We have no doubt but ere long this will be done, and in the meantime we do not tremble in the least for the result. It must result in good, for the truth rejoices in the light.

Then there is another thing to which we are constrained to allude before we begin our exposition. It is our firm conviction that it is not enough for the Church to exercise discipline in relation to those views, and even suspend from the office of the ministry those who are convicted of holding critical opinions which are not in harmony with our Standards. Sooner or later, the theories themselves must be tested as to their truth or error. Now, while we maintain that the administration of discipline in such cases is most necessary and right, and while we insist that "the Scripture as interpreted by our Standards" forms the law by which the man accused must be tried and judged, still, in our opinion, the Church will make a great mistake if she thinks that she has done all her duty, or really removed all the danger to which she is exposed at the hands of these radical theories of Higher Criticism, when she has simply cast out the heretic. The theories themselves must also be refuted, and conservative scholarship has a work of great importance to do in this field. Unless such scholarship can really confirm and justify the judicial action of a Church court, that action itself will be robbed of much of its rational value and moral force. For if the discipline be administered and the theory be not refuted, then the alleged heretic becomes an ecclesiastical martyr before the world. We believe in the judicial procedure, and have no sympathy with the popular sentiment against "heresy hunting," but we believe also in the valuable service which the conservative higher critic is to render in the refutation of false and dangerous theories on this field.

It goes almost without saying, therefore, that it is very necessary, for our ministers, as far as possible, to have intelligent views in regard to these theories; for, in case any man is put on trial in one of our Church courts, touching these theories, it would be a great pity if the accused could, with any show of reason, turn on his judges and say that they did not really know enough about these theories to judge intelligently in regard to them. How strong an argument is there also in all this in favor of sound and ample scholarship, sanctified to the Master's service; and what an impulse this view should give to some of our bright young men to bend every energy to render this valuable service to the Church.

CHAPTER II.

EXPOSITION — PHILOSOPHICAL PRESUPPOSITIONS.

THE last chapter began the work of exposition. It was, however, entirely introductory in its nature. It pointed out the fact that the modern advanced theories of radical critics originated beyond the sphere of the reverent critical study of the Scriptures, and that these have been, without proper passport or naturalization, brought within the borders of Christianity. It is legitimate, therefore, for conservative criticism to regard the radical theories as aliens, till they can by proper credentials fully vindicate their citizenship. On this position we shall insist constantly.

In the same chapter it was also contended that some intelligent acquaintance with these radical theories, on the part of our ministers especially, is of great moment at the present day. It cannot be either safe or wise to ignore these speculations, when we find them spread broadcast among intelligent people by various channels. Above all it was held that not only should discipline be administered in regard to those who hold views not in harmony with the Standards of the Church, but the theories themselves must be refuted by the methods of sound scholarship. Then it was also hinted that those who may have to sit as judges in cases of discipline involving these theories should, in some reasonable measure, be qualified for this service.

In this chapter we begin the task of formal exposition of advanced criticism. We seek first of all to discover and exhibit some of the underlying principles which the radical theories assume.

At the beginning of this work it was pointed out that the essential feature of radical or destructive criticism is not that it handles the topics of Higher Criticism, but that it deals with them in a certain way. In other words, it is the *principles* which it assumes, the *presuppositions* which it makes, and, above all, the *methods* as well as the general *spirit* according to which it does its work, that constitutes the real nature of the advanced criticism now under review. Hence, the indictment of conservative criticism is not against Higher Criticism as a legitimate branch of sacred learning, but against the principles and presuppositions, and above all, against the methods, of that school of Higher Criticism known as radical, rationalistic, or destructive. This chapter undertakes to exhibit some of the principles and presuppositions to which afterward we shall take exception.

In the first place, advanced criticism is dominated by a philosophy, and it makes the principles of this philosophy its main presuppositions. We are only saying what every well-informed scholar knows when we assert that Biblical Criticism, as well as Theology, in Germany, has been dominated by philosophy. The philosophy which for over a generation in the early part of the present century exercised almost unlimited sway over Criticism and Theology, was that of Hegel. Even if we admit what seems to be the case, that at the present time there is a tendency to return to some of the fundamental positions of the Kantian philosophy, still the fact remains that we can truly say that modern rationalistic criticism in Germany was rocked in the cradle of the Hegelian philosophy. And the English-speaking critics who have imported radical methods and theories into Britain and America, should be required to show cause how they can safely adopt these methods and hold these theories, and yet pay no regard to the philosophical principles from which these theories have descended by direct succession. Even to repudiate the parentage is no guarantee that the nature of the child has undergone radical change.

In these articles we cannot enter upon any exposition of the Hegelian philosophy. It would be no easy task to do this, and it is scarcely necessary for our present purposes. It will suffice to say that Hegel's philosophy is an elaborate system of absolute idealism, which really constitutes a scheme of idealistic pantheism. It differs from the pantheism of Spinoza in positing, as the basis of all reality, absolute spirit, or unconscious impersonal reason, in the place of the infinite, eternal, and all-embracing substance of the scheme of Spinoza. It is worth while remarking that the system of Herbert Spencer has points of contact with that of Hegel, unlike as they are in many respects. Both are monistic, and so allow only one real existence, and leave no place for a personal Being who transcends the universe. In both systems there is what may be termed an eternal evolutionary process. In Hegel's system we have that eternal process of "becoming," by means of which in the sphere of nature and of spirit the absolute idea of unconscious reason seeks to realize itself; while in Spencer's scheme we have that eternal movement of the homogeneous, by means of which the heterogeneous in actual definite material forms is brought into existence. Hegel's principle of eternal logical process is an idealistic evolution, and Spencer's principle of eternal physical movement is materialistic evolution. Thus extremes meet in philosophy; and the scheme of Hegel is that with which radical criticism is connected.

At this juncture it is certainly striking to observe again that pantheism and Higher Criticism of an advanced type seem frequently to run side by side. From the history sketched in previous chapters, we saw that Spinoza was among the very first to broach the theories of the Old Testament literature and religion which are adopted by modern radical critics. In his hand pantheism and advanced criticism are side by side. And, as already stated in this chapter, they reappear side by side, during the last fifty years in Germany, in the idealistic pantheism of the Hegelian philosophy.

Now, sometimes strange coincidences do happen, but we can hardly believe that it is a matter of chance that Spinozism and the Higher Criticism are found together in the seventeenth century, and that Hegelianism and Higher Criticism flourish side by side in the nineteenth century. We are strongly inclined to believe that there is some natural and inner connection between these two things which justifies the statement already made, that modern radical Higher Criticism is dominated by Hegel's philosophy. We might go further, perhaps, and make good the position, alike from the nature of the case and from the facts of history, that idealistic pantheism really underlies the radical literary and historical methods and theories of modern critics. In Hegel's "Philosophy of History," we have simply an application of his idealistic pantheism to explain, in an evolutionary way, the universal history of the human race. In Wellhausen's "History of Israel" we have a special application of the same principles to the origin and growth of the Jewish nation and religion. Our first point of exposition is thus brought clearly out, that modern radical criticism is the child of a spurious idealistic pantheism.

It is only fair, however, to add in this connection that many radical critics may be totally unconscious of the real parentage of their theories. Some of our English-speaking critics may not be conscious of the philosophical principles which are involved in their critical methods. Some of these writers may indeed entirely repudiate all sympathy with these philosophical views, and yet if the theories are the product of such principles in the hands of those who invented them, we are justified in looking with distrust upon the same theories, even in more reverent hands. It may turn out that the founders are consistent; and the logic of events may show that false principles will surely work out their legitimate evil results. We, at this stage, simply express our suspicion of the philosophy which, if it has not begotten radical critical theories, was certainly associated with their infancy.

In the second place, advanced Higher Criticism virtually sets aside all belief in the supernatural, or so minimizes it as to entirely empty it of real meaning. This follows naturally from the preceding consideration already adduced. The idealistic pantheism which underlies these radical, critical theories is at the same time an evolution or development which takes place in a purely natural way according to the necessary laws of logical processes. Hence everything comes into existence in a purely natural way. There can be no supernatural revelation, no miracle, and no real incarnation in the advent of Jesus Christ. Human history even is ruled by the same necessary natural law, and if we call anything in human history supernatural, we either use the term in a sense which is not Christian, or we may apply that term to all events in the line of universal history. Grant idealistic evolution as a natural development, and all events are either natural or supernatural according to the sense in which the words are used. Niebuhr, the historian, virtually applied this principle to the history of the Roman Empire, and we have the wonderful results in his remarkable "History of Rome," where the history is an ideal structure rather than a faithful record of facts.

In like manner, when the advanced critics, a few years ago, in Germany, began to apply the same historical methods, based on the same philosophical principles, to the narratives of the Scriptures, it would not have required the gift of prophecy to predict the result. We would expect that the attempt would surely be made to explain the religious ideas and institutions of the Jews in a purely natural way. So we find the radical theorists maintaining that the national history and religious ideas of the Jews form but a part of that wider and entirely natural process, in which, by an eternal process of "becoming," the absolute idea was seeking to realize itself in the progress of human history. Hence, it was consistently contended that the *cultus* of the Jews, as well as of other nations, arose and was developed in a natural and necessary way. It is abundantly evident that the sure result of all this would be to reduce religion in every form to pure naturalism, and in this case the religion set forth in the sacred Scriptures was doomed to the same fate. The supernatural must go. This is the fiat of the philosophy of radical criticism.

To show that our position at this point of the exposition is neither fanciful nor far-fetched, we need only mention the fact that Kuenen, in the introductory chapter of his work on the "Hexateuch," takes special pains to say that he sets aside all belief in the supernatural, and in the special inspiration of the Scriptures. If Graf and Wellhausen do not openly take the same position, the manner in which they deal with the questions of criticism, and the results they reach, clearly justifies the same verdict against them in regard to the repudiation of belief in the supernatural.

These, then, are two of the principles upon which radical criticism is built. Two others remain for presentation in the exposition of our next chapter. In closing this chapter, we are surely justified in sounding a warning note against the hasty adoption of a style of criticism which involves such anti-Christian principles. Even if the English-speaking critic, in all honesty of purpose, thinks that he can adopt these methods and results, without also taking the principles, he may find that he has simply attempted the impossible, and succeeded in being illogical.

CHAPTER III.

EXPOSITION — PHILOSOPHICAL PRESUPPOSITIONS CONTINUED.

MANY of the readers of our last chapter were no doubt ready to regard it as rather philosophical, but on reflection we are convinced that they will admit that any exposition of advanced criticism must exhibit the philosophy of which it is the child. In that chapter two of the underlying principles of this school of criticism were set forth. The idealistic evolution of the philosophy of Hegel, and the denial of the reality of the supernatural, are the two assumptions which were considered. Two others at least remain for discussion in this chapter.

The third presupposition is that the old view of inspiration, sometimes termed the traditional, must be discarded. If the supernatural has no validity, of course inspiration can have no place. If the Christian religion with its literature be simply a naturalistic growth, then revelation in any real sense is impossible, and inspiration cannot have any reality. In general, the advanced critical theories seem to come into conflict with the ordinary and generally received views of inspiration. This is usually confessed by those advanced critics who are striving to retain the supernatural in their system, in such a way as to show that these theories necessarily bear hard on a consistent doctrine of inspiration. One will tell us that verbal inspiration is no longer tenable, in the light of assured results of modern criticism. Another will assert that the concept only, and not the language form, can be inspired. Still another will argue for an inspired nation which produced the religion and sacred literature set forth in the Holy Scriptures. In every case the revolt against a definite scriptural doctrine of inspiration is evident.

In regard to this general presupposition, it is not easy to give a brief and simple exposition which will do justice to various phases of advanced criticism. Thorough-going, destructive critics, like Graf, Kuenen, and Wellhausen, openly and boldly reject the doctrine of the inspiration of the Scriptures in any proper sense. According to their view the Scriptures are excellent sacred literature, but they are in no special manner different from the Zend Avesta or the Vedas. They may even go so far in some cases as to say that the Scripture narratives do not really differ from the Annals of Tacitus, the Memorabilia of Xenophon, or the History of Thucydides. Then, having made this assumption, these radical critics proceed to deal with the Scripture narratives *as if* they were in no respect different from other good or even sacred literature.

Without any exaggeration, we can very safely say that the advanced school in the persons of its continental leaders, is at open war with the historic doctrine of the inspiration of the literature of the Christian system. If the doctrine of inspiration be accepted even in words, it is so entirely changed as a matter of fact that it is no longer the same. If the shell remains, the kernel is gone.

It is only fair to remark here that not a few advanced critics profess to retain the doctrine of inspiration while pursuing their critical methods. They maintain that the doctrine of inspiration is not really involved in the controversies in the field of criticism, and that the doctrine can in no way be injured by radical methods and reconstructive conclusions. Robertson Smith took this position in the controversy which resulted in his removal from his Chair at Aberdeen. He maintained most strenuously that the investigations of Higher Criticism did not interfere in the least with the validity of the doctrine of the inspiration of sacred Scripture. Briggs endeavored to stand on the same ground with but indifferent success. Driver and Cheyne in Britain, and Harper in this country, all find themselves compelled to modify their views upon inspiration. They, too, take up the cry that the old views of inspiration are no longer tenable. They tell us again and again that the assured results of modern criticism demand that the doctrine of inspiration must be recast. In every case the result of the recasting is that the new form is decidedly lower and less definite than the old.

Now it is to be greatly feared that those who are attempting to hold a reverent doctrine of inspiration, and to follow out radical methods, are much less logical and consistent than those who throw inspiration overboard entirely at the outset. To our minds it seems clear that if the philosophy and radical critical methods of the continental leaders in this movement be adopted, there is neither a place nor any need for the doctrine of inspiration. How long Anglo-Saxon critics shall succeed in retaining any satisfactory view of inspiration while using the methods of their Teutonic teachers remains to be seen. We are seriously inclined to think that inspiration will vanish entirely, and leave nothing behind but the human husk in which the divine kernel was lodged. In any case to assume and follow principles in criticism which are in conflict with hitherto accepted views of inspiration, is inadmissible at the outset.

In many respects we regard this as one of the chief dangers which arise from the adoption of the methods of radical criticism with its reconstructive theories. If we, in the legitimate work of Higher Criticism, feel ourselves perfectly free to play fast and loose with what purports to be historical facts, and to re-arrange the chronological order of the events according to philosophical presuppositions,

PHILOSOPHICAL PRESUPPOSITIONS. 99

or in accordance with subjective opinions, we simply make it impossible to retain our belief in the general contents of the Scriptures as infallible and authoritative. This procedure at once renders a definite doctrine of inspiration impossible. Each critic makes or unmakes his Bible till there remains no "word of God which liveth and abideth forever," upon which men can with confidence rely.

A true doctrine of inspiration must be determined by the claims which the Scripture makes for itself, and by the facts which the sacred record actually contains. This once ascertained, our whole study of the questions which Higher Criticism handles should be pursued, mindful of the fact that Scripture actually possesses the peculiar quality which inspiration denotes. This being the case, we cannot so separate inspiration and Higher Criticism as to find our results in the latter in no way affecting our views in regard to the former. What we have already said in regard to the pressure which the advanced critics find imposed upon them by their theories, to recast, modify, or abandon the doctrine of inspiration, is full proof of this assertion. The sound position, as we understand the case, is to deal with the sacred Scriptures by the *same* literary, historical, and grammatical methods as we would with any other literature, but at the same time to remember that we ought not to treat the Scriptures *as if* they were the same in all respects as other literature. The factor which inspiration denotes cannot be ignored. To adopt critical methods and results which shut out inspiration, is the great danger to which we are exposed by the results of advanced criticism. Consistent radical criticism sets inspiration aside at first, while advanced reverent criticism adopting unsound principles will surely find itself, in spite of its reverent protestations, led by the logic of events to the repudiation of inspiration in any proper sense.

The fourth and last general assumption which radical criticism makes lies in its general theory in regard to the origin and growth of religion. That theory is the evolutionary or naturalistic type. In its continental propounders, advanced criticism holds the evolutionary theory in regard to all the religious systems in the world. These systems, we are assured with a great deal of learning and much authority, are all the natural products, some lower, others higher, of the religious instinct in man. So in like manner with the religious system set forth in the Bible ; it, too, is the product of evolution. By slow degrees, through many ages, the development of the natural religious sentiment of human nature has been going on, and the last mature product is the Christian system with its wonderful literature. Why it has ceased with this system, or whether the evolution shall yet go beyond it, we are not told.

Accordingly, the first forms of all religions were the lowest and crudest, and the law of development was progress from the simple to the complex, from the lower to the higher. Thus the Jewish system was a gradual growth from polytheism with tribal deities to monotheism with the one living and true God. In like manner, the ritual and legislation of the religion of Israel expanded from very simple forms to increasing complexity, all by a natural law of evolution. At length, in the fullness of evolutionary time, the Christian system appeared as a decided advance, and it stands as the ripest fruit of the development process. And we are assured that the process of upward movement is still operative, and that Christianity may in due time have to give way to "the religion of the future," which will be still an advance on Christianity, although a purely natural product whose general nature we are left to surmise for ourselves.

Then since the religion itself is a purely natural evolutionary product of humanity endowed with the principle of progress, the literature of this religion is also the product of evolution, not of divine revelation and inspiration. The sacred Scriptures are but the product of the various stages of religious attainment to which the people producing the Scriptures had reached. These Scriptures simply register the religious ideas of the ages in which they were produced, instead of being the product of divine interposition. The Jewish Church and nation and the early Christian Church produced the Scriptures entirely, whereas the true view is that the Scriptures and their contents produced the Jewish and the early Christian Church. This inversion of the order is a serious matter.

We add that while some advanced critics may repudiate all sympathy with this evolutionary principle in the growth of religion, yet the fact cannot be ignored that in the hands of the founders of these radical theories it plays a very important part in their speculations. That there is need for the utmost care here on the part of conservative criticism is self-evident. Divine development is one thing, but natural evolution is another. Criticism must respect the former, but dare not parley with the latter.

CHAPTER IV.

EXPOSITION—THE METHODS OF ADVANCED CRITICISM.

FOR two chapters we have been making some exposition of the underlying principles of the school of radical criticism now under discussion. Four of these principles or assumptions were briefly expounded. In the course of the discussions it has appeared that the philosophy of idealistic pantheism, the denial of the reality of the supernatural, the repudiation or modification of inspiration, and the acceptance of the evolutionary explanation of religion, constitute the main principles and underlying assumptions of advanced or rationalistic criticism. This is specially true of it in its birthplace, and as held by its leading advocates.

In this chapter we pass on to deal in a general way with the *methods of procedure* adopted by advanced criticism. And at the outset, we wish to say that the space at command in a brief work of this kind, renders it quite impossible to go into much detail in our exposition. It will be entirely out of the question to attempt to follow the various views of different writers in this school of criticism. This would be an almost endless task, for there are now so many of these writers, and there is such a lack of agreement among them in regard to almost every point raised in the controversy, that to gather the consensus of opinion is a difficult undertaking in itself. We must consequently content ourselves with general expository outlines of view in treating of their methods.

In the discussion upon which we now enter, it is well to remember that the principles and methods of rationalistic criticism are applicable to the whole of the Scriptures. At one time the battle may be hottest on the Old Testament field, and at another on the New. A generation ago the forces were in fierce conflict on the New Testament territory. Driven from that region, they marshaled their forces and entered on a campaign against the Old Testament. Here the conflict is now waged with the utmost vigor and determination, so that the clash of arms is heard on every hand. The forces of advanced criticism now claim some important victories, and at times show a rather boastful spirit. That they shall be able to hold all the positions they think they have surely captured, remains to be seen. That they have really made all the conquests they claim to have made, may be seriously questioned. That internal dissensions in the ranks of advanced criticism already exist, and shall soon weaken the force of its assault, may be asserted with some confidence.

At present, the real center of conflict is on the Old Testament field, and it gathers around the religion and sacred literature of the Israelites. This being the case, we shall perhaps best expound the methods of advanced criticism at present in vogue if we deal directly with these methods as exhibited in their treatment of the origin and growth of the religion and sacred books of Israel. Adopting this general course, we shall have to deal at length with the ritual and legislation of the Pentateuch, and with the prophets and their work in the expansion of the religious ideas and practices of the people.

At the very outset we signalize the fact that the *methods* of advanced criticism to a large extent constitute *a theory*. In the procedure of nearly all its original exponents, a theory is assumed and brought to the facts, instead of the theory being made the adequate philosophy of the facts. Much that has been said in two preceding chapters justifies this statement. The radical critics come to their task with a theory in regard to the supernatural, in reference to inspiration, and concerning the origin and growth of religion. Then with this theory in their hands, they proceed to deal with the Old Testament history and religion. Professing to be above all else historical critics, we find them openly ignoring the simple historicity of the Old Testament Scriptures, and proceeding to reconstruct the history, not in the light of profane history and monumental evidence, but according to the stern conditions of a mere theory. While they insist repeatedly that they only of all the critics are the true scientific critics, we often find them pursuing entirely unscientific methods in dealing with the way in which the idea of deity, the expansion of ritual, and the complexity of legislation actually developed in Israel. Here, again, as we hope afterward to show at some length, we find the advanced critics dominated at every turn by a theory. To them, it often seems that a theory is more real than a fact, somewhat after the manner that Bishop Berkeley, as a philosopher, would have us look upon the reality of the material objects of the outward world. One of the curious things in the whole controversy on the field of Higher Criticism is the coolness with which what the advanced critics term the traditional views are set aside, and the confidence with which theories, which at best are but working hypotheses not yet proved, are put in place of these views. In some cases the advanced critics are so possessed with their theories that the assumption seems to be unconsciously made by them that they are the only scholarly critics, and that their criticism alone is scientific and worthy the notice of thinking men. At the outset of our exposition of the *methods* of advanced criticism, we point out the fact that they are to a large extent hypothetical, or a set of theories, which are boldly propounded as the assured results of modern criticism, which all men of enlightened scholarship must accept on pain of exclusion from the guild of "competent scholars."

Perhaps the remaining part of this chapter can best be devoted to a brief bird's-eye view of the general type of theory in accordance with which the contents of the Old Testament religious system must be recast. In presenting such a sketch we do not follow any single writer closely, but attempt to present a general view of the Graf-Wellhausen hypothesis as set forth by its original authors in part, and as modified by its English-speaking modern exponents in part.

As already indicated the debate gathers round the history of Israel, and the origin of that nation and of the system of religious ideas and practices contained in the Old Testament Scriptures, and especially as found in the mature Levitical system. There are three distinct factors to be briefly presented here. These are the national, the religious, and the literary features of the religion of Israel. Hence the rationalistic critics have a theory of the nation of Israel, of the growth of their religious system, and of the production of their sacred books. Throughout, the supernatural is denied, and an explanation by means of mere naturalistic development is attempted. This is the *theory*.

In regard to the origin and development of the nation, the call of Abraham, if it has historically any reality, was nothing more than a natural migration. Even Cheyne in some recent utterances seems to be prepared to go as far as Stade, a professedly rationalistic critic in Germany, who regards Abraham as a somewhat mythical personage. In general, the radical critical theory looks upon Israel as the product of a number of wandering tribes, rather than of a divine call of, and care for, one family. These tribes, not very different from other tribes of that age and locality, settled in Canaan, and, instead of remaining distinct and making conquest, mingled with the tribes already settled there. By degrees a process of natural amalgamation took place, and the result was the production of the Israelitish people. In the early ages there were no such national features as are denoted by the twelve patriarchs, the sons of Jacob and the sources of the twelve tribes of Israel. The tribal idea came into existence later on, and had really no definite form at first. It will thus be seen that so far as the origin of the nation is concerned, there is no essential difference between the beginnings of Israel and the genesis of the peoples and nations of Greece and Rome from various scattered elements gradually combining together in a natural way. This conception or theory of the nation lies at the basis of the entire radical critical scheme.

In the second place, regarding the origin and development of religion, the radical critics maintain that at first a form of polytheism prevailed. The chief deity was Jehovah, or Jahveh, who was not really regarded as the one living and true God, but rather as a tribal deity, not unlike Baal, Molech, and Dagon. It was only by slow degrees that monotheism was developed, and polytheistic elements were eliminated. Not, indeed, till the age of the prophets did ethical monotheism appear, and it was only after the Exile that monotheism became the fixed form of belief in Israel.

In like manner, the ritual and legislation in the Mosaic system only came gradually into existence and observance. At first, sacrifice was simple, and the form of worship was not elaborate. The rites and ceremonies were not essentially different from those of the tribes round about them. Early customs, primitive observances, and legendary ideas by slow gradation grew into more definite form. These customs gradually rose into legislation, simple rites by degrees became elaborate ritual, and primitive modes of worship slowly expanded into the elaborate system of mature Mosaism. In this way, an attempt is made to give in a purely natural way an explanation of the rise and elaboration of Mosaism into Prophetism, and of Prophetism, in due time, into Judaism. The legislation was prior to the ritual, and the prophetic element was before the legislation. The order, therefore, is not the law and the prophets, but the prophets and the law. And last of all comes the mature Levitical code. By slow degrees, through nearly a thousand years, from Moses to Ezra, all this development occurred.

Then, in the third place, in regard to the production of the sacred books, the radical theory has its views quite in harmony with what has just been stated. Moses wrote little if anything of the books associated with his name. Perhaps part of the covenant code, as it is called in Exodus, was from his hand, but the literature of Leviticus and Numbers was not produced by him. The simple rites and customs spoken of under the previous head had developed into ritual and legislation before the literature describing these matters took its rise. It was only about the eighth century B. C., when the prophets appeared, that the literature began to take definite shape. But it was not till after the period of the Exile and Ezra that most of the Old Testament literature took its definite final form. True, there were portions of the literature extant before, but it existed in scattered documentary form, as the critics say, and, by the slow processes of the crude literary methods then in vogue; it took its final shape only a few centuries before the Christian era.

Such is a brief general description of the methods of the advanced critics, which at the outset we describe as *a theory*. In the above sketch we are satisfied that the position of radical criticism has not been overstated. Our readers must be convinced that even this statement is sufficient to show how radical and destructive of the ordinary views this theory is. By its very boldness and show of learning, it commands attention, and its proposed reconstruction of the religion of Israel demands careful examination. The next chapter will open up further particulars in regard to it.

CHAPTER V.

EXPOSITION — DOCUMENTARY HYPOTHESIS.

IN the last chapter emphasis was laid upon the fact that the general procedure of advanced critics was really a *theory*. They have a theory of the Jewish people, of the way in which religion developed among them, and in regard to the mode in which their sacred books were produced. This theory, we are convinced, is not the one which the biblical writers themselves seem to have held, but it is rather a mere hopothesis, according to which the claim is made that the history and religious system of the Scriptures must be reconstructed. We make bold to say, even in the face of high claims to the contrary, that the general methods and results of Higher Criticism of the radical type have not yet been removed from the region of unverified hypothesis. It might even be debated whether they constitute a verifiable hypothesis.

At the same time we are convinced that as a theory, with certain supposed conclusions established, it touches vital features of the Christian system, as we understand that system. The general theory of the Jewish nation, ritual, and literature set forth in the last chapter, fully justifies this statement. Advanced critical conclusions, in our judgment, are not merely certain views regarding the mode of the composition, the age, and the authors of certain books; but these conclusions imply a definite theory in regard to the Christian system in general, and in relation to the inspiration of sacred Scripture in particular, which, so far as we can see, cannot be reconciled with sound views of Christianity, and which are, therefore, full of serious danger to some of the essential factors in that system of religion which, we believe, exhibits the supernatural as its unique and distinguishing feature. The situation is one, therefore, which surely demands careful study.

In continuing our exposition of the methods of radical criticism we shall, in this chapter, seek to give some brief explanation of the manner in which the so-called *documentary hypothesis* is used in support of the advanced critical views now under discussion.

In general, this hypothesis maintains that the Scriptures as we now have them did not take their present form all at once. They were compiled by various authors, rather than composed by the writers to whose hands they have been usually ascribed. It is assumed that in early times there existed a considerable mass of disconnected narratives and traditions among the people who composed the Jewish nation. There primitive documents and traditions were used by the writers of the books of Scripture, and so by a gradual natural process the literature was constructed to a large extent out of pre-existent documents. In like manner, it is further assumed that the books thus produced did not take their final form till much later than the dates ascribed to them by the ordinary historical view. In harmony with this general supposition, we are assured that the authorship and date of the several books is a matter of little moment; and, indeed, radical critics seem to think that anonymous authorship gives a higher value to the books in question. One of the many curiosities of the methods of advanced criticism appears in this connection. It consists in the strange anomaly of the critics' ability to tell us all about how the books were compiled, and what parts belonged to this author and that, to this age and that, and yet at the same time the names of the various authors or compilers are not given by the critics. It does seem strange that the wonderful critical insight which enables the critic to resolve a book into its simple elements, and the ability which qualifies him to reconstruct the composite literature in a new mould, are not also sufficient to enable him to give us the names of the authors of the various sections of the literature, or even of the completed compilations. If the names of the writers are hypothetical, may not their supposed work as authors and compilers be also hypothetical. In other words it is *theory* throughout. But we must give more particular

DOCUMENTARY HYPOTHESIS. 115

explanation of the way in which the doctumentary hypothesis is utilized in favor of the radical critical position.

The different critics vary in view in regard to the several documents which enter into the structure of the books in their final form. We can, therefore, only present the general features of the theory. Since the critics are ignorant of the names of the authors of the various elemental factors in the Old Testament books, they have been compelled to invent symbols and figures to denote these unknown literary personages. We shall now describe these in order to show how the documentary hypothesis is used in the methods of advanced criticism.

The symbol "J" is taken to represent certain original writings which were drawn up by an author called the Jehovist, or by a series of writers who used the name Jehovah to denote the Deity. Those passages of the Old Testament in which this name is applied to the Almighty are, quite irrespective of the subject matter with which they deal, ascribed to this supposed author or series of writers. The radical critics go through the Scriptures, especially the Pentateuch, and cull, transpose, and cast out words and phrases as they think the documents written by "J" require.

The symbol "E" is used to denote the author, or set of authors, who wrote those passages in which the name Elohim is applied to the Supreme Being. These passages are perhaps among the very earliest which enter into the composition of the Old Testament, and they are supposed to have been written by a writer, or series of writers, who, for some reason, preferred the name Elohim to Jehovah. The first chapter of Genesis is a good example of this document which has come to us from the Elohist.

Then, some critics speak of "J E" as another and a later writer, who, with "J" and "E" both before him, combined them, or as a separate author who preferred the compound name Jehovah-Elohim for the Deity. In either case, those parts of the Old Testament wherein there occurs this double naming of the Deity, are to be ascribed to an author or series of authors distinct from the Jehovist and Elohist writers. Hence, wherever this name so occurs, it is assumed that another set of authors produced these documents. The most of the second chapter of Genesis is a good illustration of these particular composite documents produced by "J E."

Another important set of the producers and compilers of certain parts of the Old Testament is denoted by the symbol "D." This symbol represents the Deuteronomist, and the main substance of his literary materials appears in the Book of Deuteronomy. Of course this writer, or series of writers, went over the writings of the previous authors, as above described, and modified them, adding certain parts ; and thus the critics profess to be able to point out all through, what parts belong to each author. The substance of the Deuteronomic legislation came in this way into existence, but at a much later date. The time usually ascribed is a little before the days of Josiah, 625 or so, B. C. Some of the critics have such remarkably keen insight that they think they can discover several Deuteronomic writers, and these are denoted by the additional symbols "D_1," "D_2," "D_3." As thus decorated with learned suppositions, the writings of some of those advanced critics look like treatises on higher mathematics where certain symbols are used to denote unknown quantities. The work of the Deuteronomist and his assistants is important inasmuch as it appears in the production of a large part of the books of Moses as they are called.

A still further symbol used is "P." This expresses those portions of the Old Testament which are supposed to have been produced by a set of priestly scribes who lived about the time of Ezra, and who did so much to develop the mature Mosaic ritual. Large parts of Genesis, Leviticus, and some sections of Numbers, are due to these priestly scribes. Hence the literature of the developed scheme of sacrifice and ritual comes into view, together with historical additions. It is usually held that the religious rites and beliefs herein set forth actually came into existence by a process of codification prior to the writing of the books giving an account of them. These writings were gradually developed in the ages before Ezra, and the priestly set of writers reduced the regulations to writing, and retouched further the previous writings, so as to produce the highly composite result which this part of the Old Testament presents. Here also, in addition to the original "P," there was a number of other priestly writers, who were imbued with the priestly spirit, and these are denoted by the symbols, "P_1," "P_2," "P_3." Thus much of the elaborate ritual and legislation, showing an increasing monotheistic conception of the Deity, and exhibiting a growing tendency to one central place of worship, comes into existence according to the opinions of radical critics. In the hands of "P," and his co-laborers, the system of mature Mosaism eventually appears.

Finally, the last symbol which the radical critics employ is "R." This symbol denotes an author, or a set of writers, who lived and labored after the Exile, and whose labors put the Old Testament into its final canonical form. These writers, for several of them are assumed, went over the whole Old Testament Scripture already in existence, and re-edited it. The history was filled in, the monotheistic idea of God was made definite in its ethical form, and the one central place of worship was insisted on by the Redactors. The later books and many of the Psalms only came into existence at that time, and are due to the labors of these nameless

Redactors. The various writers who belong to the school of "R," are further denoted as "R_1," "R_2," "R_3," as in preceding cases.

The sketch of the various documents as represented by the symbols described, is entirely general in its nature. According to the theory they represent, the Scriptures become a curious piece of complicated mosaic, or, as some would prefer to say, a section of stratified rock made up of primary, secondary, and tertiary formations. If details of any particular phase of the critical theory were given, much more definite statement than we have space for would have to be made, in regard especially to the relations between the various documents and the part to be assigned to the Redactors. We would have to point out that "P" uses Elohim also as far as Ex. 6 : 3. This is based upon the recent view that "P" and "E" together constitute what was by the earlier critics taken to be a single document, and called the "Elohist." Some suppose that in Gen. 2 : 3 the Elohim was inserted by the Redactors, and that the original document belonged to "J" not to "J E," this latter symbol being used ambiguously, and its scope quite doubtful. This is specially the case in Wellhausen's theory. Then "R" should scarcely be placed on the same plane as the other symbols, for the reason that the Redactors did not so much produce any new documents, as recast and edit already existing materials. But the whole subject of the documents and their supposed combinations is an endless one. Still it is by this method that the critics suppose that the Old Testament was produced.

It is in this way that the *documentary hypothesis* is used to support the theory of composite authorship and evolutionary origin of the Old Testament writings. In accordance with this theory, re-arrangement of the literature is needed in order to get the true view of the way in which the literature was produced, and of the manner in which the religious system was developed. The treatises of the radical critics, setting forth the application of the documentary theory, are curious specimens of literature and will make capital material for coming critics to exercise their skill upon. The elaborate tables in Driver's book on "Introduction," seem to us to be not so much bold strokes of critical sagacity, as elegant and suitable epitaphs prepared beforehand for theories which we feel sure are doomed to early death. So, also, the attempt of Brown and Driver to construct a Hebrew lexicon in which they use the symbols above described to designate certain sections of the Old Testament, seems to us to be a great risk of money and of literary reputation. If in coming years other critics rise up who know not the present critics, and if these critics invent new and original symbols, the present learned lexicon will become meaningless and useless. It will then be in order to revive it reverently from its sleep in the library, and lay it away tenderly in a case in the archæological section of the museum.

But this chapter must close. It has sought to show how advanced criticism uses the *documentary hypothesis* to support its radical position. Further exposition will be given in the next chapter.

CHAPTER VI.

THE THREE CODES.

THIS chapter continues the exposition of the *methods* of procedure which advanced criticism follows in seeking to establish its radical conclusions. In the last chapter a brief account of the way in which the *documentary hypothesis* is used to support these conclusions was given. Four or five different documents, with perhaps a dozen minor ones, are supposed to have been used in the production of the Scriptures as we now have them in the Old Testament. In the absence of any knowledge of the names of the authors or compilers of these documents, the radical critics have invented certain symbols by which to denote these unknown literary personages. The result is curious, if not entirely fanciful. If we were to place these symbols side by side, so as to denote the sum total of the documents which enter into the Old Testament Scriptures, we would get a result something like this: "J"+"E"+"JE"+"D"$_{1+2+3}$+"P"$_{1+2+3}$+"R"$_{1+2+3}$= O. T. This is the mathematics of the methods of the radical critics, and it expresses the results of the use of the *documentary hypothesis* in a nut-shell.

It is, however, still an unsolved equation in the hands of radical criticism.

In this chapter we take up another line of exposition, not entirely distinct from the one followed in the last. This line consists in giving some explanation of the several supposed codes of ritual and legislation which the Mosaic system exhibits as viewed by the advanced critics. Just as they maintain that a variety of documents makes up the Old Testament literature, so they reason at great length in favor of a succession of different codes or schemes of worship, sacrificial rites and legal requirements. In some respects this is the very core of the radical theory. The hypothesis of the codes relates to the way in which the essential elements of the religion of Israel were actually developed. The method in which the literature was produced is determined largely by the deeper question of the way in which the religious system of the Israelites came into existence. If it came into existence in a purely natural way, as the radical critics argue, then the simpler codes will be first and the more elaborate later on. If the religion of Israel is the product of special divine communication, then a different, likely the reverse, order may be expected. Consequently, the hypothesis of the diversity of codes of ritual, worship, and legislation is a fundamental position of the advanced critical theory. Such being the case, careful exposition is needed at this point.

The section of the Old Testament which lies specially before us in the exposition of the diversity and successive origin of the several codes of the Israelitish religion is the Pentateuch. The advanced critics discover, as they think, from a careful scrutiny of the vast mass of legislation in these five books, several distinct strata of laws and directions in regard to religion, which have come successively, and perhaps at considerable intervals, into existence. The law was not *given* by Moses, but it was *produced* by evolution. Through three or four distinct stages this evolution can be traced, according to the critics; and each stage has left the proof of its existence in the literature as described in the last chapter. With microscopic care, the vast mass of regulations regarding the sacrifice, worship; and practical life of the Israelites is studied, and out of the supposed chaos, order is brought by means of the hypothesis of the codes. These codes must now be described.

In the first place, there is what is called the Covenant code. This is the earliest and simplest of them all, and shows the nature of the cultus, or worship, in its first or germinal stage. This code is supposed to be the form of ritual and legislation set forth in the Jehovistic historical sections of the Old Testament literature. In particular, it is set forth in Exodus 20-23. In this passage we have the Ten Words or Torah, as they are sometimes called, as the main factor in the Covenant code. In addition,

THE THREE CODES.   125

there are certain directions regarding the kind of altars which are to be built, and about certain sacrifices to be offered thereon. There is, however, no elaboration of priestly ritual. Then, there is a mass of legislation in reference to practical matters, such as masters and servants, husbands and wives, parents and children, neighbors and their relations in many respects, and the various feasts to be observed through the year. There is not much about the priests and their duties, but a great deal concerning the people and their relations to each other in this code of the Covenant, and the critics enlarge upon these things at great length.

But there is no settled agreement among the critics in regard to what after all is to be included in the Covenant code. Some would include Exodus 24, also, where we have an account of the time when Moses, Aaron, and the seventy elders were commanded to go up into the mountain, and of Moses alone being asked to come near unto God; and when we are also told that they obeyed, and Moses remained for forty days and forty nights in the mountain with God. But others are inclined to the opinion that the Exodus form of the Torah should include only the statement of the ten commandments. This, strictly speaking, is the Covenant code, according to some critics. Then, too, there is great diversity of view among the critics as to how much Moses had to do with the production of this code. Some only allow that it is Mosaic in spirit, but assert that Moses did not write this Torah; others hold that the code and its record alike are from the hand of Moses. Hence, even in regard to the precise form and contents of this simplest of all the codes, there is no substantial agreement among the critics in regard to the main factors of the theory at this point.

In the second place, the critics describe what they call the Deuteronomic code. In a general way, the contents of this code are found in the book of Deuteronomy or the second law. ·The radical critics point out how this book differs from other parts of the Pentateuch, especially from Leviticus and Numbers. There is, they say, no elaborate scheme of ritual and detailed legislation enjoined upon the people, or described as actually in vogue among them at the time that Deuteronomy was written. Emphasis is laid upon the fact that the graded priesthood is not prominent, and that prohibitions against idolatry abound in this code. There are laws in it which are not found in any of the other codes; and, in general, it is concluded to be essentially different from the others. Here, again, there is no agreement in regard to important details, but into an exposition of these particulars we cannot now enter. The general position of radical criticism is that on many essential points this code differs so greatly from the others that they cannot all be the product of one founder, or of the same historical period. The critics also differ

THE THREE CODES. 127

greatly in regard to the time when this code originated, and as to the author, or authors by whom it was written. In general, it is held by most advanced critics that this code came into existence a short time before the days of Josiah, and its literature is contained in the documents known by the symbol "D," described in the last chapter.

In the third place, the critics describe another important code under the title of the Priestly code. The record of this is found in the latter part of Exodus, in the whole body of Leviticus, and in a considerable portion of Numbers. There is much diversity of view in regard to what portions of these three books set forth this code. Some would confine it largely to Leviticus, others would embrace a good deal of Exodus, and nearly the whole of Numbers. Speaking generally, this code comes to us with documents known by the symbols "P" and "R." In this code mature Mosaism in the full sense of the term appears. Here the complete priestly system, the elaborate ritualistic scheme, and the detailed legislation are unfolded; and one central place of worship, definite monotheism, a complex sacrificial system, the annual feasts, the tabernacle service, and all the other elements of mature Mosaism originate. The critics also are in no agreement in regard to many important particulars regarding the contents of this code. Some think that Ezra and others of his day had the chief part in this important task. Others argue that the men who lived after the Exile, and who completed the Old Testament canon, had the most to do with the unfolding of the cultus of this code, and in the production in its final form of the literature in which it is described and enjoined. Others think that the regulations of this code may have been in existence and operation in earlier times, but were only reduced to writing after the Exile ; and then the record of the whole, together with the history accompanying it, was thrown back and connected with the name of Moses. But on this boundless sea of critical speculation we cannot now embark.

These, then, are the three chief codes which advanced criticism sets forth as contributing the contents of the religion of Israel, and as indicating the manner of its production in a natural way. We have the Covenant, the Deuteronomic, and the Priestly codes. In connection with the last, some recent critics, as for example Driver, are inclined to make a separate code of Leviticus 17-26, in which there seems to be a special collection of laws enjoining holiness on the part of the people. This they would call the *Law of Holiness*, and give it an origin of its own, distinct from the Priestly code, in the very heart of which it stands. But further exposition of the hypothesis of the three codes, important as it is in itself, is impossible.

To conclude this chapter we only add that the advanced critics argue not only for the existence of these three codes, but that they are so divergent in their contents as to be from different hands, and to be the product of ages widely apart. We also emphasize the fact that the critics are greatly divided in regard to the *order* of these codes. The Wellhausen school hold the order as above expounded, but another school, represented by scholars like Schrader and Dillmann, advocate the view that the Priestly code goes before the Deuteronomic in the order of time. That this is a clear concession to the true position is evident, and this order certainly calls for a revision of the fundamental positions of the Wellhausen theory. Again we see that the outstanding feature of radical criticism is diversity of opinion.

CHAPTER VII.

SOME GENERAL FEATURES.

In the last chapter the hypothesis of the *three codes* was explained. It was seen that advanced criticism argues that there were three distinct codes of ritual and legislation in the development of the religious system of the Israelites. These three are named the Covenant, the Deuteronomic, and the Priestly codes. They are held to be so different in their contents, and so widely separated in time that they cannot have come from the hand of any one man, nor have all appeared in the era of Moses.

In this chapter some further exposition of the reasonings by which this position is supposed to be established will be given. In our judgment, the hypothesis of the three codes is one of the central factors in the advanced critical position. Some are inclined to regard the Deuteronomic code, and its place in the order of development, as the significant element in the controversy. Doubtless, much may be said in favor of this latter view, but it may suffice for our present purpose to look upon the supposition that the three distinct codes came into existence centuries apart, as the very heart of the radical theory. This being the case, some further explanation of this position and of the reasons adduced in its support is necessary.

In the first place, on the literary side, the critics deal at great length with the general literary features of the supposed diverse documents in which the laws of the several codes are set forth. With the most wonderful critical insight that ingenious literary criticism has ever exhibited these documents are inspected and dissected. Then, with unbounded confidence, judgment is pronounced upon words and phrases, upon idioms and style ; and various attempts are made to reconstruct the dissevered fragments in accordance with the scheme of the three codes above described. As the result of this critical treatment of the literary sources of the various codes the critics conclude that no sort of unity or contemporaneousness among them is possible. The style of the literature of the several codes varies so much that diversity of codes and composite origin of the writings, is the only hypothesis which meets the case, in the judgment of the critics. We have sometimes wondered whether it has ever occurred to the advanced critics that they first assume these codes, and then proceed to discover as they think, diversity of literary features to such a degree that they cannot observe any solid basis of unity between them such as enables the critics to reunite what by hypothesis they have needlessly severed into artificial parts.

In the second place, the critics lay much stress upon the fact that there are what they regard as significant omissions in some of the codes, and some even go so far as to say that there are inherent contradictions in the statements of the several codes. According to the critical view on this point there are laws and regulations peculiar to each of the codes. The Covenant code is the simplest in its form, and it is also the most general in its contents. In it there is no gradation in the priesthood, as high priest, priests, and Levites, nor is there any elaboration of the ritual and sacrificial scheme. It is in the Deuteronomic code that we find distinct directions in regard to a central place of worship, while the Covenant code, so the critics say, allowed worship at many local shrines. So, in like manner, strict monotheism as an actual fact, with all the elaboration of the mature Mosaic scheme, did not appear till near the time of the Exile, if not, indeed, after that great event. Now, these and many other features of diversity in the contents of the supposed codes are taken by the advanced critics to prove their theory of different codes, widely separated as to the date of their origin. Our space entirely forbids an adequate exposition of this particular point, so we must be content with these general explanations.

In the third place the advanced critics give very great prominence to what took place in the days of Josiah and during his reform. For some time prior to this reform under Josiah the people, so the critics say, had been observing the substance of the regulations found in the Deuteronomic code; but about the days of this good young king the influence of the prophets had been sensibly felt in the development of religious ideas, and in the production of the literature of that code. Accordingly, what Josiah did was not so much to effect a reform in religion so as to lead the people back to the old but forgotten law and ritual, but his great work was rather to originate a new onward movement in the religion of Israel. It is from this view-point that the "book of the law" given by Moses, which was found in the Temple and read before the king, is to be understood. Hilkiah and Shaphan were, in the opinion of the critics, the authors of this book of the law, so that it was not the product of Moses, nor of the Mosaic era.

Here critical opinion follows two lines in regard to the precise manner and purpose of the production of this book of the law. Some regard it as a *praxis*. By this term the critics mean that what had hitherto been practiced among the people in the way of religious observances, was reduced to written form for the first time by Hilkiah, Shaphan, and others of Josiah's day. Hitherto it had been unwritten practice or custom; at Josiah's day it became written law or code. In this way the book of the law found in the Temple is to be understood, and the name of Moses was attached to it to give it additional authority, as tradition had previously associated the unwritten *praxis* with the name of this great personage of the Exodus.

The other critical view of this book of the law is to the effect that it was a *reform programme*, rather than an unwritten *praxis*. It looked to the future and affected it, rather than to the past in the way just described. Hilkiah and other earnest men of the time of Josiah drew up the contents of this book of the law, and promulgated it as a scheme according to which the religious life of the people was to be shaped. They brought it to the king, then a young man, and presented it to him as the book of the law which had Mosaic sanction, but did not fully inform him of the true authorship of the book. In this way the critics maintain that the reform under Josiah was inaugurated, and the Deuteronomic code came into actual observance in connection with that reform. In either case the Deuteronomic code is not Mosaic. It is a *praxis*, or a *programme*, so say the critics. In the criticisms to be offered in future chapters, much will have to be said in regard to advanced critical opinion regarding what took place at the time of Josiah, and in the age immediately prior to it.

In the fourth place, the advanced critics enlarge on the things which took place in the days of Ezra, and in connection with the restoration from the Exile. In some respects, this is the most important of all the epochs in the history of the religion of Israel, according to the advanced critical view. It was at this time that the fully developed Mosaic system appeared. Prior to the deportation of the people in the great captivity, there had been a general observance of many of the things contained in the Priestly code, described in the last chapter, but it had not been reduced to written form. Idolatry was spoken against by the prophets of the days before the Exile, ethic monotheism was fully developed, worship at one central sanctuary was enjoined, and a very elaborate priesthood and ritual had come into existence. During the Exile, according to some critics or just after it according to others, Ezra and the earnest spirits associated with him drew up the complete Priestly code in written form. This was observed by the people after the Exile, and soon developed into the rigid and formal Judaism of the century prior to the advent of Jesus Christ. Half a dozen chapters would not suffice to give more than a summary of all that the critics have set forth at this point, in their advocacy of the reconstructive theories. This exceedingly meager statement, however, must suffice, and it may be enough to provide at least a basis for future criticism.

In the fifth place, many of the critics give a peculiar place and prominence to the wonderful vision of Ezekiel, which is found in the closing chapters of his prophecy, beginning with the fortieth. The scope and imagery of this vision need to be pondered by the hour to feel its grandeur and power. In a vision, Ezekiel, under the guidance of some angelic being, beheld a magnificent city. In it there is a splendid temple, most elaborately furnished in every respect for its purpose, and ornamented most exquisitely. Then in the temple there is an altar, forth from which a stream of water flowed that soon became deep and wide, making fruitful all the regions whither it flowed. Then, in connection with the temple, there is an elaborate sacrificial system exhibited, and even a division of the land among the twelve tribes is alluded to. But the whole account of the vision must be read to be appreciated in this connection. No brief description can do it justice.

Now, one influential school of radical critics lays much store by this vision. They make it the transition between the Deuteronomic code and the Priestly code. Here they say we have all the elaboration of the ritual and sacrificial system which is found in the Priestly code, and that originated about the days of Ezra. From the way the critics speak of this vision, we almost receive the impression that they regard it as having actually existed as an observed ritual system among the people, whereas there does not appear to be the slightest evidence that the contents of this vision were ever observed, or even intended for observance, under the religious system of Israel. Nay, more, perhaps a strong case can be made out for the opinion that the contents of this most wonderful vision have meaning only under the assumption that the so-called Priestly code was an actual fact among the people prior to the days of Ezekiel. Our criticism later on must lay hold of this point, and sift the critical view carefully.

In the last place, this may be the best stage to note the fact that the advanced critical theory maintains that the idea of the *Tabernacle* and its ritual had no existence till about the Exile. There may have been, we are told, some sort of a tent, and perhaps the ark or something like it, but the notion of the Tabernacle with its services as set forth in the Priestly code did not exist in the early stages of the history of the religion of the people of Israel, but it was an inference from the Temple. Instead of the Temple being an expansion of the Tabernacle, the Tabernacle was the Temple in miniature and projected back to the days of Moses in an idealized form. So in like manner the great Annual Feasts are of quite late origin. They do not date back to the era of Moses, and they do not originate from his hand. Both of these points will come prominently forward for criticism ere long in the course of this work. In the meantime this mere statement must conclude this chapter. The exposition will be completed in one or two additional chapters; then the real task of the critical examination of these radical theories will be begun.

CHAPTER VIII.

THE HISTORY.

THE last chapter opened up several lines of statement and reasoning by means of which the advanced critical theory, and especially the hypothesis of the three codes, is supposed to be established. At the close of the chapter two important factors in the critical theory were merely mentioned. The one was the contention that the Tabernacle did not exist, and the other the supposition that the great annual feasts did not originate, or at least come to be generally observed, till late in the religious history of Israel. This follows naturally from the terms of the theory. The Tabernacle service and the annual feasts were connected specially with the Priestly code. This code, according to the critics, did not come to be generally observed till about the time of Ezra, which of course was quite late in the history of the national life of Israel. Consequently, the idea of the Tabernacle succeeds the Temple; and the great feasts, such as the day of Atonement, the feast of Tabernacles, and the day of Pentecost, had no place in early times. These factors of the theory will call for careful examination when we proceed with our criticism.

THE HISTORY. 139

This chapter deals with a single additional feature of the advanced critical position. That feature relates to the explanation of the history which we find running side by side with the ritual and legislation of the several supposed codes. The question here is this: How is the history to be accounted for and harmonized with the outlines of the critical theory? This, moreover, is one of the real difficulties with which the radical theory has to contend. That theory claims to be strictly historical; and yet, when from the basis of its theory concerning the development of the religion of Israel, it attempts to interpret the history of the Old Testament Scriptures, it is compelled to rearrange the materials of the history in such a way as to be really a reconstruction of the history, in accordance with the necessities of the theory. This chapter can only give a few hints as to the way in which the history is treated by radical critics.

In the first place, the critics point out what they suppose to be two concurrent lines of history quite distinct from each other, running through the Old Testament. In the one *prophetical*, in the other, *priestly* features are prominent; and, while concurrent, the critics often represent them as inconsistent at various points. Speaking generally, the former consists of the books from Genesis to the end of the book of Kings; the latter includes Chronicles, Ezra, and Nehemiah. In both cases pre-existing materials in documentary form have been used.

The one corresponds in general with the "J E" and "D" narratives, and is built on the Covenant code ; the other agrees in the main with the "P" and "R" narratives, and implies the existence of the Priest's code. There is endless diversity of opinion among the critics concerning the details of view in regard to these two lines of history, as they suppose them to be, and in regard to the relations which they sustain to each other.

In the second place, the critics make another important three-fold distinction which bears upon the historical sections of the Old Testament. They distinguish between the *origin* of the ritual and other laws, the *codification* of these laws, and the *writing* of the law books in their final form, with the history interwoven. With more or less definiteness, the critics make these distinctions. Sometimes the distinction is two-fold instead of three-fold in the hands of the critics. According to this view, the origin and observance of the laws are distinguished from the literature in which the record of these laws and ritual requirements is now found. But the latest form of critical theory announces the distinction to be three-fold in its nature as above noted, and it makes use of this in its effort to explain the historical narratives which run parallel with the ritual and legal factors of Mosaism.

According to the first of these stages of codification, the laws and ritual observances are viewed as coming into existence among the people but remaining in a disconnected, unclassified form, and entirely unwritten. They were little more than customs made definite and handed down in a traditional way. In the second stage, these laws or customs, having gradually become numerous and complex, were reduced to an orderly form, and classified into what are called distinct codes by the critics. At this stage, some of these laws thus codified were reduced to writing, but were not yet arranged in a connected narrative. In the third stage these laws, as codified and traditionally observed, were reduced to definite written form in later times. This was done partly for the convenience of the priests who were to administer the ritual, and partly to fix definitely the priestly form of the *cultus* as distinguished from the prophetical.

It is with the last stage that the historical elements of the Old Testament are, the critics think, to be largely connected. There were certain traditional factors in the life of the nation, historical in their nature; and in the later stages of the national career these were written up long after the events happened, and in this way the history is to be regarded as a later semi-ideal product. It was not written at the time, but most of it took written form long after the events actually happened, just as the laws were reduced to written form long after their origin and observance. In subsequent criticism this is a point to which careful attention must be given.

In the third place, in regard to the precise mode by which the history came to be thus written, the advanced critics have some remarkable things to say. It is at this point, too, that their theory suffers one of its severest strains in relation to the history which it must in some way account for. If the narratives which have, as they now stand, such definite historical form, came into existence at the late date which the radical theory asserts, then the question is, how is the clear-cut historical form of these narratives to be accounted for? The strain upon the theory at this point is so great that the critics are driven to remarkable expedients in order to give a show of plausibility to their speculations. A mere statement of these expedients will not only exhibit what they are, but also indicate how great is their weakness and superficiality, and will show how desperate the necessities of the theory which calls for such support must really be.

Some critics give what may be called the *traditional* explanation of the historical narratives. By this explanation it is set forth that the main body of the events actually happened, but that the knowledge of them was for many ages handed down from generation to generation by oral tradition. Like all tradition it would undergo certain modifications and receive constant additions, so that in the later ages of the national life of Israel there existed a great body of tradition which was then reduced to written form. But in it all, while there may have been a basis of fact, there was also much that is traditional if not mythical in the supposed historical sections of the literature of the Old Testament as it now stands.

Other critics give what may be called a *fictitious* account of the historical sections of this literature. In it we have, according to this view, not a record of real events, nor the later transcription of oral tradition, but an entirely fictitious product. According to some, this fictitious history was produced by later post-exilic scribes to fill in the legal and ritual codes, which had by that time been reduced to written form. By other critics, the free and natural play of the imagination of these scribes working alongside of the ritual system, produced these historical narratives. In the former case, they are intentional, and in the latter, spontaneous products. But in both cases their real historicity is ignored.

That this general view of the history is revolutionary is self-evident. According to it, we have in the Old Testament not real history, but tradition or fiction, or a mixture of both. The supposed persons, places, and events are imaginary, not real; and the alleged authors of these books never wrote them, but their origin is due to the mythical instinct, poetical genius, or dramatic power of some nameless scribes who lived and wrote in the degenerate era after the Exile. Were it not that we find this theory set forth in professedly learned books, we could not have believed that such a forced interpretation of what seems to be very distinctly marked history, was to be discovered anywhere. But we have it here in the writings of radical critics.

It is in this connection that emphasis is laid by some critics upon what is called *pseudonymous authorship*. Others call it *literary fiction*, which they claim was a common thing in those early days when no copyrights existed. According to this view, these later authors to whose hands the historical books owe their origin, attached the names of some great men of ancient times to their writings to give them more weight. These ancient and weighty men are *represented* as speaking and acting in the historical events described. The name of Moses, in a somewhat dramatic manner having acquired much traditional prominence, was the name to which much of the history, and most of the ritual system associated therewith, were ascribed. Thus, by a pious fraud, called by the milder name of *literary artifice*, or by the pretentious term *pseudonymous authorship*, the historical setting of the ritual system of the religion of Israel is sketched ; or perhaps we ought more truly to say, that the history was dramatized. Of this we shall have something to say in future criticism upon this topic.

The result, then, is that the history no longer remains history. At best it is but tradition ; perhaps most of it is fiction, as some say. The history is the *free creation of post-exilic times*. Under

THE HISTORY. 145

the exigencies of the radical theory of the ritual system, the history is first destroyed in order that it may be rebuilt in accordance with the architectural requirements of that theory. The narratives are not, as they now stand, a correct expression of the development of the religion. Hence the narratives must be reconstructed to fit the theory. The work of editing and re-editing has gone on, till almost all semblance of historical material in the narratives has passed away. That such an attempt should be made in the name of *historical* criticism to explain Abraham, Moses, Joshua, David, Josiah, Isaiah, Hosea, Ezra, and other personages, must ever remain as one of the literary wonders of the nineteenth century fitted only to be classed along with Donnelly's Baconian theory of Shakespeare.

CHAPTER IX.

THE PROPHETS AND THE PSALMS.

WE are now nearing the end of the exposition of the literary and historical methods of advanced criticism which it was our purpose to make. The last chapter sought to show how the history of the Old Testament is to be understood in the light of the radical critical theory. This chapter will seek to explain how the *prophets* and their work are to be understood, and the place which the *Psalms* are to be given by the theory under consideration. With this chapter the direct exposition will thereby be concluded.

In a former chapter it was hinted that the advanced critical theory puts the prophets before the law, and so would read, "The Prophets and the Law" instead of "The Law and the Prophets." The real meaning of this must now be unfolded, and in this way the view of the place and the work of the prophets in the development of the religion of Israel may be best exhibited, according to the critical theory now under consideration.

In the first place, in order to understand the position of advanced criticism in regard to the prophets, we must keep in mind what that criticism holds in regard to the general status of religious ideas and observances at the time when the great prophets, who have given us important written prophecies, lived and exercised their religious influence. In general, the critical theory maintains that the religious life and the ritual observances of Israel were a gradual growth. At first it was the simple worship of Jehovah, offered at many places throughout the land. In this early stage the rites were few and by no means elaborate. Perhaps some of them were forms of *nature* worship which were by degrees adapted to the religious conditions of Israel in Canaan.

Then, in particular, when the early *writing* prophets, as they have been called, appeared, they found the religious ideas of the people quite crude, and their *cultus* far from mature. The great work of these prophets was to do much toward the advancement of the religious life of the people, rather than to bring the people back to an old ideal from which they had wandered. Previous to the *writing* prophets there had been *oral* prophets in earlier days, who partly paved the way for the work of the men whose prophetic words have been put on permanent record in the Scriptures. Such were Elijah and Elisha.

But the men who effected most for the religion of Israel were men like Hosea, Jonah, and Amos, in the kingdom of Israel; and like Isaiah, Jeremiah, Ezekiel, Micah, and Joel, in the kingdom of

Judah. Through the teaching of these men it came to pass that ethical monotheism was developed, and that the people were led to worship at one central sanctuary. At this time, also, and by the influence of the *writing* prophets, the legislation and ritual system came into general observance among the people. Prior to their time, this elaborate ritual had really no existence, and the teaching of some of these prophets is such as to discountenance, rather than to foster the observance of the ritual system. These prophets lived from six to eight centuries, B. C., and from their writings the critics argue that the Deuteronomic and especially the Priestly codes were not then in existence, for these prophets say little about the contents of these codes. Arguing from the fact of this silence, they hastily conclude that these codes were not in existence to be observed by the people. These prophets paved the way for the developments which took place in Josiah's day and at the time of Ezra, when the law, in its fully developed form, came into existence and observance. Of course different critics give different explanations of the influence of these and subsequent prophets; but the main thing to keep in mind is that the advanced critical theory denies that the priestly code, or Torah, was in existence eight centuries B. C., that is, in the days of Hosea and Amos in particular. And on the other hand, the theory asserts that the law, in its completed form, at least, came into common observance, if not into actual existence, only after the prophets had exercised their potent influence. The law is thus post-prophetic.

In this way the meaning of the statement that the order of development is from the prophets to the law, not from the law to the prophets, is to be explained. The real authors of the mature Mosaic system are the prophets, especially the *writing* prophets. Directly, by their teaching, they developed monotheistic belief and unity in the place of worship. This centralization was naturally followed by an elaboration of ritual at the one sanctuary, and thus, indirectly, the prophets prepared the way for the introduction of the priestly or Levitical code. It will be observed that this order of the prophets and the law, grows out of the necessities of the theory of three codes, which puts the Priestly code about the days of Ezra, when the great work of the prophets was virtually over. How curious the procedure of the critics is at this point! Again and again the attempt is made to construct an elaborate theory on a very slender basis of fact; and having propounded the theory, it is even used to determine what the facts must have been.

In connection with the work of the prophets another thing may be mentioned. The advanced critics make their analysis of the prophetical writing very much as they do of those writings which exhibit the several codes. Prophecies which have been supposed all along to be complex wholes are cut in twain, or if the case requires, are divided into a number of sections. Thus Isaiah is severed into two, and Zechariah is served in the same way. The supposed dates are assigned to the several parts, even though the critics do not know the names of the authors of the later sections. Daniel is carried away forward to the era of the Maccabees, as also are other writings which have always been regarded as pre-exilic. The reason given for this high-handed critical procedure is that these parts of the prophecies, such as the later part of Isaiah and of Zechariah, could not have been written until the ritual of the Priestly code had come into vogue among the people, as it did only a short time prior to the Exile. Then, too, passages or allusions in the prophets which seem inconsistent with the terms of the radical theory, are branded as interpolations from a later age, and so are cast aside. In a word, the *theory* must rule, no matter what becomes of the facts in the case.

A few paragraphs must be added in regard to the way in which advanced criticism deals with *the Psalms*. As the theory was pushed forward to its logical conclusion by its advocates, and especially as the evolutionary principles involved in the hypothesis of the three codes were unfolded, it soon became evident that the profound religious ideas and sentiments expressed in the Psalter could not be easily harmonized with the stage which the evolution had actually reached in the days of David, the period when many of these very Psalms are supposed to have come into existence. This was long prior to the days of Josiah and Ezra, and it was not till their days that the religious system reached its maturity, according to the radical critical view. The religious contents of the Psalms are consequently before their proper time if we retain the commonly received view that most of them belong to the age of David and Solomon. Hence the critics place the origin of very many of these Psalms at or after the time of Ezra.

But the skill and boldness of the critics are quite equal to the task thus presented. Instead of revising their theory in such a way as to do justice to the religious elements in the Psalms, they put the Psalms on the rack of radical criticism. The result is that the Davidic authorship of most of the Psalms is denied, and the date of their production is brought down to the period after the Exile, and subsequently to the elaboration of the Priestly code and its observance among the people.

Indeed, some of the critics go so far as to say that none of the Psalms were put in their present form till after the days of Ezra. Such critics merely admit that the simple elements of some of them may have existed among the people prior to that great epoch, just as the elements of the Iliad of Homer existed among the early Greeks. These elements were not yet crystallized, but only held in solution in a mythical age. But the critics contend that the Psalms, as we now have them, are of late date, which means that they must have come into existence chiefly after the Priestly code was produced. The critics, in this connection, like to speak of the Psalter as the *praise book* of the second Temple, forgetful of what the history says about the musical service of the first Temple being very extensive, and entirely consistent with, if indeed not requiring the contents of the completed Psalter. Here the order which the advanced critics give us is the Prophets, the Law, and the Psalms, instead of that which our Lord himself suggests in the last chapter of Luke, as the Law, Prophets, and Psalms. But the theory demands this order, and so the critics insist that the theory must rule. Later on, we shall examine the position of advanced criticism in regard to the Psalms, and we may then be able not only to set it aside, but also to find materials in those Psalms which are admitted to be of Davidic origin to refute the hypothesis of the three codes, which, as we have already said, is the very heart and core of the whole critical structure.

Thus we see more and more clearly the tendency of the advanced critical theory to bring down to as recent a date as possible all those parts of Scripture, whether they be history, prophecy, or Psalm, which contain distinct allusions to the contents of the Priestly code. The reason for this obviously is that by hypothesis it is assumed that this code did not come into existence till about the time of the Exile, and in the light of this assumption the parts of the literature which contain these allusions must either be interpolations by some late hand, or the whole writing is of more recent origin than is generally supposed.

But at this point our exposition of the methods of advanced criticism must close. The reader is doubtless glad that we have brought him to the end of the long and tedious journey, even if he has been willing to follow us thus far through the mazes of the various factors of the critical theory. This exposition nevertheless has not been sufficient to set forth the theory with details of illustration. Still we would fain hope that what has been said may provide a sufficient basis upon which criticism may be intelligently made for the reader. With the next chapter we invite the reader to embark with us on what may be termed a voyage of observation and discovery, in the course of which by careful inspection we hope to find many things new and old which may enable him to make a careful estimate of the critical theory, and which may help him to obtain an intelligent view of the main defects by which it is to be distinguished.

PART IV.

CRITICAL EXAMINATION.

CHAPTER I.

PRELIMINARY.

WITH this chapter we begin the careful examination of the advanced critical theory, whose main positions have been somewhat briefly explained. Three chapters have been devoted to introductory explanations; in five, a short history of radical criticism has been given; and in nine chapters an attempt has been made to give an exhibit of the chief features of radical criticism. With these chapters before us, we venture to hope that we are in a position to enter upon a careful review of this particular critical theory. To do anything like justice to this task even in a brief and popular manner nearly a score of chapters will be required. The present one will be almost entirely preliminary in its nature.

In dealing with this very extensive and many-sided subject, it is of much importance to have a clear conception of the *methods* according to which a proper examination of advanced Higher Criticism should be pursued. In previous chapters, we were careful to ascertain the *methods* of advanced criticism; and now, when we undertake to enter upon the review of that criticism, we ourselves should be exceedingly careful to adopt and follow sound *methods* of procedure. We should keep in mind the adage about people who live in glass houses throwing stones. If, therefore, we may cast some stones in the way of criticism of the radical critical theory, we would take diligent care that our general method is not like a glass house.

In the first place, we wish to emphasize our firm conviction that the present current debate between conservative and radical criticism is one of great importance in itself, and of vast moment to the Christian system. Between the two opposing schools of criticism the difference is, in our judgment, not merely one of details but of underlying principles. The attitude of the two schools is essentially different in regard to the view held concerning the very foundations of the religion of Israel. If conservative views in regard to the place of divine revelation in originating this religion must be given up before the victorious march of the radical theory, then an entire reconstruction of the essential elements of the Christian religion, including even its divine redemptive system, will have to be made. The conviction grows upon us that, while this assault upon the very foundations of the history and religion of Israel as involving a supernatural factor may not be entirely new, yet it is an attack made by naturalism or rationalism in a new manner which calls for new refutation. Let no one, therefore, make light of the issues involved, or be indifferent to the outcome of the controversy, for very much depends upon it.

In the second place, the questions involved are, we believe, far deeper than even the important matters of authorship and literary style. The critics in certain quarters have dwelt so much on discussions about style, idiom, and other literary features in determining the authorship and date of the several books of the Old Testament, and consequently of the origin and date of the religious contents of these books, that undue prominence has been given to this, which at best can only be a superficial feature of the religion of Israel. High claims are made by some of the critics for scholarship and critical insight, and others of them in a rather haughty way warn the conservatives that unless they possess similar learning and insight, they are not qualified to give a judgment in the case. The advanced critics only are the scholars! The poor conservatives are regarded with sentiments something like pity, and it is plainly hinted that their learning is antiquated and quite out of style.

The problems raised are rooted much more deeply than this surface view implies. The questions which emerge are not merely concerning the authorship of the books of the Old Testament, but of the authorship of that national and religious life of the Jewish nation which made it so radically distinct from other nations. The debate has reference, not merely to the origin of writings in which this remarkable life is recorded, but it relates to the deeper problem of the origin of religion in general, and of the Israelitish religion in particular. The heart of the controversy is not reached by inspecting with microscopic care the mere literature of the religion, though we may learn much from this source. The nature of the religion exhibited in that literature, and above all, the order and principles of its development, constitute the real problem to be dealt with. If this be the true view of the case, the debate goes far deeper and is much broader than it is often conceived to be. In a word, it raises the general question of the philosophy of religion, and directly formulates the problem of the philosophy of the religion of Israel. This is the position we take in entering on the criticism of the radical theory of the history and religion of the people of Israel. It is at its roots a problem in religious philosophy which is formulated for solution.

In the third place, we shall take care that no undue assumptions are made by the critics at the outset. We have learned already how prone radical criticism is to deal in assumptions. What some of these assumptions are, as laid down by advanced criticism, we shall discuss in a subsequent article. What we here at the outset especially signalize is this, that we shall not allow without protest radical criticism to assume or deny certain things which, being assumed or denied, may necessitate some of the main conclusions of their theory. Thus, for example, we shall not allow the higher critic at the outset to assume, as Kuenen does, a certain theory in regard to the origin and growth of religion, nor to deny the reality of the supernatural in the form of revelation, inspiration, miracle, and prophecy as so many do. We shall certainly insist on these being at least left open questions till the investigation is complete, and we shall not allow any school of critics to shut the door in the face of these important elements which claim to have a place in the Old Testament Scriptures. The conservative with good grace might properly take still higher ground, and justly hold that since these Scriptures themselves claim to contain direct divine communications and other features of the supernatural, he has a right to assume the reality of the supernatural in the debate ; and, should he do this, his position is made all the more reasonable from the fact that it has been the almost uniform view of the Church. She has looked upon the religion of Israel and the Old Testament Scriptures as permeated with a divine factor in the history, the religious ideas, and the literature of that religion. The advanced critical theory is a comparatively recent thing. It was born outside the Church only a few centuries ago, it was brought into the Church less than a century since, and so it should at least have the merit of the modesty becoming its youthful years. If any party in the controversy has the right to make assumptions in this field, it is the conservative.

But we do not insist on this position at the outset. We simply content ourselves with refusing to allow the radical critic to make his denials and assumptions without question. We further give due notice that we shall feel free to sift the presuppositions of the radical critic as fully as may be necessary, should he venture to make them.

In the fourth place, we are strongly inclined to the view that there is no middle course which can be safely taken in this controversy. We doubt very seriously whether, between the radical critical theory and the historical conservative theory of the national and religious life of Israel, any compromise that does not mean capitulation is possible.

There is a tendency in some quarters to accept to a considerable extent the radical theory of the history of the national life of Israel, and of the origin and development of their religious ideas and rites; and, above all, there sometimes appears to be an *undue* readiness to accept the radical critical conclusions in regard to the production of the literature; and at the same time the hope seems to be cherished that the historic faith of the Church in the supernatural factor in the religion of Israel can be held fast. We doubt if this is possible, and are very sure that it is not necessary to attempt any such compromise in order to pursue scholarly methods. The national and religious life of Israel are so interwoven that no separation between them is possible. If the history be the manufactured

PRELIMINARY. 163

product of later times, we ask what becomes of the religious ideas with which the history is connected? Are they also manufactured? If Adam, Noah, Abraham, and Moses are not distinctly historical personages, how can we retain as real the religious truths and redemptive promises which are associated with these great names? The history and the religious systems must in the nature of the case stand or fall together, for the facts of the history are often doctrines in the concrete; and the events of the narratives are frequently religious truths of the utmost importance. We cannot deny the reality of the history without oftentimes leaving the doctrines and religious truths hanging in mid-air. This being the case, we are convinced that any concession to advanced criticism other than such as legitimate criticism approves cannot be safely made. We proceed with our criticism, therefore, assuming the strict historicity of the narratives of the Old Testament Scriptures. If this be not done, we cannot see how any conclusions are to be reached, for these Scriptures are our only source of information regarding the matters in question. We are convinced that this position can be safely taken, and all the interests of legitimate Higher Criticism be fully conserved.

In the last place, we believe that conservative Higher Criticism has a very important task to do in taking hold of the various lines of reasoning which the advanced critics have opened up, and following them out step by step. We may surely be pardoned for not believing in the infallibility of the advanced critics, and we shall surely be excused for venturing to deal in as fair and frank a manner as the case may require with all the facts adduced and theories advanced by these critics. This we shall do, at least until the critics at some ecumenical council announce their own infallibility, and give good proof of this by formulating the "assured results" in which modern critical scholarship rests its weary feet. We believe that along every line, conservative Higher Criticism can hold its own, if it pursues its work in a solid, thorough way. The principles involved, the standpoint assumed, the methods of criticism employed, and the conclusions drawn by radical criticism, therefore, all lie before us. And we cannot regard the conservative critic as an invader when he enters the lists on this extensive field with radical criticism in the interests of what he regards to be the true welfare of the Christian religion. Perhaps the conservative critic could justly take the position that he is simply seeking to drive off invaders who have appeared on the field in the persons of the radical critics, for their theory is certainly recent and novel. But we content ourselves with simply meeting advanced criticism face to face, and handling it by the legitimate methods of criticism. In the next chapter we begin our task directly.

CHAPTER II.

THE UNDERLYING PHILOSOPHY.

HAVING in the last chapter set forth some preliminary matters, we now enter formally on our task of criticism. In this chapter some remarks will be offered regarding the general philosophy which underlies all forms of rationalistic criticism, and whose validity, we believe, may be seriously questioned. We are convinced that the modern radical school of criticism of the Scriptures is very largely the outcome of a certain philosophical view of the relations subsisting between God and his works, and of certain assumptions concerning the mode of the divine operations in relation to the universe. At the very outset we insist that no adequate critique of radical critical theories can overlook, or afford to leave without thorough examination, the philosophy which it implicitly or explicitly assumes.

In general, the animus of this philosophy is directed towards the denial of the supernatural. As already stated in a former chapter, radical criticism, whether of the Old Testament or New, whether of a century ago or of the present day, whether within the Church or without it, always ignores, denies, or minimizes the supernatural factor, which we believe cannot be removed from Christianity without robbing it of its glory, and destroying its spiritual power.

This denial or ignoring of the supernatural has been based on one or other of two great types of philosophy. The one is a type of pantheism, the other a phase of deism. Both deal with the problem of God's relations to his works. In the religious sphere, the problem relates to the mode of the divine operations towards man, and to the manner in which God has revealed himself to those beings who possess the religious nature and sentiment as man does.

The former of these, pantheism, merges God and the universe in some way into each other. Either God is hidden in the universe, or the universe is merely the existence form of God. In either case, the distinct though dependent existence of the universe is not properly provided for. In both, the proper transcendency of God in relation to his created works is not rightly understood and expressed.

This is not the place where pantheism can be fully criticised. But we wish to have it very distinctly understood that much of the modern criticism which ignores the supernatural and seeks to give a naturalistic explanation of the religion of the sacred Scriptures, has grown out of the soil of the idealistic pantheism of Hegel. If this philosophy be allowed to dominate our methods of criticism,

THE UNDERLYING PHILOSOPHY. 167

and to guide us in formulating theories as to the origin and growth of religion, it needs no prophet to predict the result. If God is only immanent in the universe, in human history, in the soul of man, and is merely unfolding himself in a natural and necessary way therein, then everything is reduced to the category of the natural, and Christianity is only one of many forms of religious progress with nothing peculiar about it, further perhaps than that it is the best that has yet appeared. And this is precisely the conclusion which radical criticism reaches, and which it proclaims upon the housetops as the assured results of the best modern scholarship.

On the other hand, those who incline to the deistical type of philosophy put God so far away from the universe that he has now really nothing whatever to do with its history. God created it and put it under certain laws, and according to these it has ever been working out its destiny in a natural necessary way. According to this view, it is clear that the supernatural has really no place, can indeed have none. There can be no revelation, no miracle, no answer to prayer, no renewing grace. The facts of religion among men, and as exhibited in the Scriptures particularly, must all be explained as natural historical human products. In this way the results of radical criticism naturally and necessarily follow from the philosophical theory of the deist.

Of these two tendencies the pantheistic has, perhaps, the most favor at the present day, just as the deistic had precedence about a century ago. As against both we take our stand firmly on the basis of sound philosophical and biblical theism. Of the utmost importance we believe it to be, to vindicate biblical theism as against the subtle idealistic pantheism above described. Biblical theism asserts at once the transcendency and immanency of God, in relation to his works. It puts God not only before the universe as its beginning, but it makes him the ground or reason of its existence every moment. It places God not only within his works, but it regards him as God high over all, blessed forever more. By the very terms of this philosophy both the natural and the supernatural are properly explained, and a fitting place is left for every supernatural factor alike in the religious system set forth in the Scriptures, and in the spiritual experience of the truly religious life. But we cannot enlarge on this point. We charge radical criticism with holding in its hand a false philosophy of the relation of of God to his works in general, and of the method according to which he reveals himself to men in particular.

At this point, it may be well to consider further the teaching of the radical theories upon the doctrine of inspiration. In spite of all the critics say to the contrary, the advanced theories of radical criticism do, in the very nature of the case, affect the views of inspiration which can be consistently held. This does not mean that one cannot hold a proper scriptural doctrine of inspiration, and enter upon the task of the literary and historical criticism of the Scriptures. We believe that careful and scholarly criticism of the sacred Scriptures is quite consistent with the doctrine of their inspiration in the strict and proper sense of the term.

But we are firmly convinced that the results of radical criticism, and of the theories of the development of the religion of Israel which it advocates, cannot be harmonized with a sound doctrine of inspiration. If the deistical view be taken, there can be no real inspiration other than that which appears from age to age in what may be termed the natural history of religion. Any direct divine influence upon chosen men by means of which they received, and then spoke or wrote down the mind of God is simply impossible. Mere naturalism is the distinguishing quality of the religion, and human reason is the only source of authority in the sphere of religion. If the pantheistic view be taken, then in the experience and history of man the divine will is unfolded. So we are told by even such modern critics as profess to have a sincere regard for the inspiration of the Scriptures that the whole human race is inspired, inasmuch as God first reaches self-consciousness in the consciousness of man, in some such way as makes man's thought of God, God's thought of himself. This is really idolatry of a refined type, where each man virtually creates his own God. Then the only sort of inspiration, we are told, which is special in its nature is the inspiration of the whole Jewish nation. There were no chosen inspired men. The sacred books are, strictly speaking, the sacred literature of this nation. Such is the view of many modern critics.

According to this view there are really no inspired books in the proper sense. We firmly believe that it is not possible to harmonize this position with the facts and claims of the Scriptures themselves in regard to their divine inspiration. The whole doctrine of inspiration is evidently at stake in these discussions with the radical criticism. The claim of the Scripture itself, and the obvious facts it embodies require a doctrine of inspiration which cannot be made to agree with any of these naturalistic evolutionary theories of the religion and the literature of Israel.

But we cannot follow this point out at greater length. We charge radical criticism with being necessarily hostile to a sound doctrine of inspiration, and on this account are convinced that the critics cannot justly claim the liberty of handling as they please the sacred books, while at the same time they try to retain a doctrine of inspiration worthy the name.

At this point conservative criticism has a strong case against the advanced theories. If the unique character of the Scriptures as truly the inspired, infallible, and authoritative word of God be given up, serious if not fatal injury will be done to evangelical truth and spiritual religion. We need *inspired men* who have given us an *inspired book*, or set of books, which is not merely the sacred literature of the Jewish people, but a revelation from God and distinctly inspired. We are sure that the trend of advanced criticism, even in its mildest forms, is toward lower views of the inspiration and authority of the sacred Scriptures. This criticism is open to severest blame when lodged within the Church. It not only makes scrutiny of the Scriptures, but it also assails the inspired records which are the constitution of the Church itself.

It is interesting to note in this connection that, as the standard of the inspiration of the Scriptures is lowered, the degree of the inspiration of the critics themselves seems to rise higher and higher. As the authority of sacred Scripture is decreased, the authority of the critic seems to increase. Hence, there has been developed that subjectivity of the critic by which it is assumed that his opinion must be taken as of very great weight. In the exercise of this subjectivity the critic sits in judgment upon the literary form and actual contents of this book and that. He culls, omits, and modifies passage after passage, because as it stands, it does not meet the approval of his literary or moral sense of what it should be. If a passage does not fit the critics' theory as they think, they will take a good look at it, solemnly pronounce it an interpolation, and promptly set it aside. Another passage is supposed to be in the wrong place, and it is transposed according to the decision of the critic. The critic is thus much like the editor of a daily paper, who uses scissors and mucilage in culling and patching till his task for the day is complete and so much copy produced. Then whole books are severed in a very arbitrary way into two or more portions, and on a very slender basis of fact wonderful conclusions are made to rest. The theory is spun out of the critic's brain in a purely subjective manner, and when we look at the result of the spinning we find that it is but a cobweb.

Our final charge, therefore, against radical criticism in this chapter, is its subjectivity. If we were to interpret this hard word for our untrained readers, we would say that radical criticism is over-burdened with self-conceit, and weighed down with a sense of the authority of its own opinions. The whole attitude of radical criticism at this point is at fault. It is at best *conjectural criticism*, where guess-work takes the place of sound inference, and where the well-founded results of one critic cancel the equally well-founded results of another. The objective facts found in the religion and sacred Scriptures of Israel must be fairly studied by legitimate criticism, and our subjective opinions should be formulated in accordance with these facts in all critical studies.

The next chapter will deal with the philosophy of religious development associated with radical criticism. This will lead us to inquire into the soundness of its evolutionary theory of that development as it appears in the religion of Israel.

CHAPTER III.

ITS PHILOSOPHY OF RELIGION.

IN a single chapter some things have been said regarding the philosophy of which radical criticism is the child, and of the subjectivity which naturally becomes the attitude of such criticism. The fatal effects of this inadequate philosophy upon the biblical doctrine of inspiration were pointed out. Much more should have been said about this last point. That the Scriptures have a well defined doctrine concerning their own nature as inspired cannot be denied. That our doctrine of inspiration should be gathered from what the Scriptures have to say of themselves on this particular point must be admitted. Yet we find in the face of these facts that radical criticism either ignores this quality of the Scriptures altogether, or so explains it as to explain it away almost entirely. Even those critics who profess to retain the doctrine of inspiration are constantly telling us that it must be recast in order to meet the demands of advancing scholarship. Now we shall be exceedingly careful to put no barrier in the way of scholarship, and yet we must say that those methods and results of scholarship which do scant justice to the claims and contents of the

Scriptures very justly raise a suspicion in earnest minds that there is danger lurking somewhere in such critical scholarship.

In this chapter brief allusion will be made to the philosophy of the origin and growth of religion in general, and of the religion of Israel in particular, on which radical criticism rests.

In a former chapter we saw that advanced radical criticism holds and applies the principle of naturalistic evolution to the facts of the genesis and development of religion. And even critics who admit in some form the presence and influence of the supernatural factor are often strangely enamored by the magic of the word *evolution*, and evidently become unable, in some instances, to distinguish between an onward movement in religious thought and life which is entirely naturalistic, and one which is the product of real communications made by God to certain men for themselves and for the whole race.

We need not repeat what was said in a former chapter regarding the explanation which radical criticism makes of the origin and expansion of the religion of Israel. It began in its lower and rose to its higher forms. Polytheism gradually became monotheism, and simple laws and rites grew into complex and elaborate ritual and legislation, during a period of nearly ten centuries. In this respect there is really no difference between the essential principles which worked in the religion of Israel, and the principles which marked the growth of the other great religious systems which have appeared in the world. In our criticism of the radical theories this fact should be kept in mind.

We are here brought face to face with certain views which in recent years have become quite popular in certain quarters as the result of the comparative study of religions. This study, useful and helpful if rightly conducted, has, in the hands of not a few scholars, been used to level Christianity down to the plane of other religious systems. Between the religion of Israel, and that of Egypt and Chaldea, between Christianity and Buddhism, there is, according to these writers, no difference in kind. All are the natural products of the religious instinct in man working itself out in accordance with the principle of natural evolution. The religious system found in the sacred Scriptures has in it nothing essentially different from what may be found in germ at least in other systems. According to this view, the ritual and legislation of the Scriptures are to be recast to fit the theory, and the literature itself must be subjected to entire reconstruction. Upon this general position of radical criticism we make several remarks.

In the first place, it is an unfounded assumption to reduce Christianity to the category of the other religious systems which are to be found among men. Such an assumption is not supported by the facts in the case, but is the result of a preconceived theory. It would be easy to show that there are factors in Christianity which are not found in any other system. The trinitarian conception of God, the incarnation of Christ, the great redemptive scheme, and the ethical system of Christianity, cannot be the products of any amalgamation of similar factors found in other systems. A case might be made out for the view that instead of Christianity being the product of these other systems, the truths found in these systems may be a deposit from the primitive monotheism and primeval revelation from which Christianity has come by direct divine descent. More than this, even if it were made out that in some of the non-biblical religions there are factors common to them and Christianity, it would not follow at all, without clear evidence, that Christianity is simply a natural compilation of the better elements in these systems. Instead of the Christian system being a collection of *survivals* from other systems, these systems may be errant rivulets from the stream of revelation which Christianity represents. We charge radical criticism, therefore, with making a mere assumption at this point, and with giving us no evidence to support it.

In the second place, there are factors in the religious system set forth in the Scriptures which no naturalistic evolution can account for. Even if naturalism may be adequate to explain the non-biblical systems, it might still turn out that there are factors in the religion of Israel that will not be reduced in the crucible of naturalism. The lofty tone of the Scriptures, the high claim that God is speaking to men therein, the wonderful organic unity of the whole volume, the prophetic element in them, their remarkable picture of the character and government of God, the true delineation which they give of man's moral state, and the unique and potent remedy which they unfold and apply as the sure solvent of that moral state, together with a score of other factors, which might be noted, did space permit,— all stand forth as incapable of a naturalistic explanation, such as might suffice for the main features of the non-biblical systems. To rank the religion of the Bible beside the non-biblical systems, can only be done by ignoring, or overlooking, the unique factors which belong to the former. To call bitter, sweet, or the black, white, does not effect the change that the difference between these words denotes. So to rank Christianity and Zoroastrianism in the same category, can only be done by shutting the eyes willfully to the factors of the Christian system, which make it different in kind from all other systems. We charge radical criticism with unscientific procedure, which is none the less to be condemned because it is propounded with such boldness.

In the third place, radical naturalistic criticism at this point can give no satisfactory explanation of the fact that there has been an advance of religious ideas and practice among the Israelites, while nothing of the kind took place among the surrounding nations. Let the reader note this point with care. Naturalistic criticism asserts that the same principles underlie the evolution of the religion of Israel as are to be found in the religion of Egypt, of Chaldea, of Persia, or of India. The same philosophy is applicable to all alike. This being the case, we simply ask the radical critics to explain how it came to pass that by slow degrees, yet most surely, the Israelites developed ethical monotheism, and an elaborate spiritual worship, while the other nations either remained stationary or degenerated in their religous condition. Some explanation of the facts, even on the critics' own showing, must be given, and we call for a sufficient cause to account for the admittedly diverse effects or results.

It will not do to assume that the Semitic genius of the people explains it, for there were other Semitic peoples who did not bring forth the same fruitage of religious advancement. It will not do to assume some inherent superiority in the people, for in many respects other peoples of that age were as likely as Israel to produce high religious results, as, for example, the Greeks. Nor will it suffice to assume that environment accounts for it, for the potent influence of environment would have to be proved as a fact, and if proved, the result would still leave the question of the adjustment of the environment unsolved. We revert to our question again, and challenge radical criticism to give a better account of the *cause* of the development of religious ideas and life among the people of Israel than the one which it gives of itself. Some explanation of the difference between Israel in this respect and the nations round about for a period of ten centuries must be given. We postulate, as against naturalistic evolution, the presence and potency of the Spirit of God, working in and through selected persons of that chosen nation, as a full explanation of all the facts of progress exhibited in the religious thought and life of Israel, and as the true and adequate philosophy of the difference between Israel and other nations in this respect. We shall hold by this explanation, at least till radical criticism can supply a better. This we have no expectation of beholding in our day, but we shall leave our challenge open on this point.

In the fourth place, the law of purely *natural* religious evolution among men is *degeneration*. Here the radical critics generally fail to take properly into account the facts and effects of sin as moral evil on the human race. It may be laid down almost as an axiom that, owing to the blight which sin has brought upon the moral and religious nature of man, the law of his moral and religious progress on the merely natural plane, must be retrogression. Historically, this can be abundantly proved alike from secular and sacred history.

Witness the degeneration of the people before the Deluge, the declension in a few generations from the knowledge of God which all men possessed in Noah and his family after the Flood, and even the frequent falling into idolatry of Israel during its strange career, as abundant proof of this sad fact.

Then, if we enter the field of ethnology we find that social and moral degeneration seems to be the law of nature, and that wherever advance appears, it can be traced to contact with the stream of the supernatural in some way. Modern savages are not the prototypes of primitive men. They are the product of natural evolution, working according to the law of degeneration. In the field of comparative religion this same law is repeatedly illustrated. The widespread tradition of a golden age when men dwelt at peace with each other and in harmony with God, and when even nature was never angry, but heaven and earth in beneficence smiled upon men, means much in this connection. The fact that the older beliefs and practices of pagan nations, as represented by their earlier traditions, are often nobler and purer than those of the present time, cannot be overlooked here. In Egypt, in Chaldea, in Persia, and India, did space permit, facts could be adduced to show that the law of natural evolution is degeneration, and wherever an upward step has been taken, this is clearly seen to be due not to the race uplifting itself, but to the divine Hand reaching down to raise it up and lead it on. But at this point this chapter must conclude.

CHAPTER IV.

GENERAL HISTORICAL DEFECTS.

Two chapters have been devoted to the consideration of some philosophical aspects of radical criticism. Its underlying philosophical principles, and its philosophy of the origin and growth of the religion of Israel were discussed in these chapters. In both fields, especially in the latter, the discussion was far too brief. Only a few points of a general nature could be suggested. Our firm conviction is that the philosophy of religious development which radical criticism adopts and argues from is utterly defective, and we regret that our space renders it impossible to exhibit its many defects more fully than the last chapter enabled us to do.

In this chapter we pass from the domain of philosophy to the field of history. We shall test the theory at several points by the assured light which the well ascertained facts of history shed upon it. That this line of criticism is exceedingly important is indeed self-evident. The Scriptures which set forth the Christian system contain a great deal of history. In a certain sense they are a history. The facts of the history are often the vehicles for the communication of the will of God, and the revelation is thus imbedded in a well defined historical basis. This feature of Christianity renders it capable of clear historical tests, and gives its historical evidences immense value. It also enables us in turn to test those theories which radical criticism propounds by the facts of a history. If we find, therefore, that those theories run counter to the well ascertained facts of the history, then we are in possession of a potent weapon for the refutation of the radical critical theory. If, in like manner, we find that radical criticism subordinates the facts of history to the terms of its theory, or contents itself with a defective philosophy of the facts of history, then we shall be justified in rejecting the theory on historical grounds. Two chapters will be devoted to these historical inquiries. This one will present general features, the next will take up some particular considerations.

Concerning the general historical features of the religion of Israel by which radical critical theories may be tested, we must first understand clearly the precise sense in which the revelation unfolded in the Scriptures is historical. Radical criticism regards the Scriptures, with all their contents of history, ritual, and legislation, as the natural historical product of the Jewish nation. These Scriptures, according to this view, are historical in the sense that they are the products of the times in which they were produced, and that they simply register the stage of religious development reached at any particular time. The view presented is that the people of Israel produced the Scriptures, whereas the true view is that the Scriptures, together with the revelation which they set forth, produced the nation and Church of the theocracy.

Over against this view of the historicity of the contents of the Old Testament Scriptures we maintain the view that while these Scriptures are imbedded in history, and associated intimately with the successive stages of the history of Israel, yet they are not the mere product of the people, age after age, among whom they were produced. All along there was a divine factor coming in upon the age, and through chosen individuals communicating to the age something new which the age itself could never have discovered nor produced, and which is the cause of the onward and upward movement that appears in the development of the religion of Israel. It is in this sense that revelation is historical and progressive. Just as in nature the divine agency is necessary to cause the organic to come in upon the inorganic, the rational upon the organic, and the moral upon the rational, so the divine agency is the real and requisite causality which lies back of every true advance in religious activity, during the ages when the Scriptures were produced. Both in nature and revelation there are progress and a continuous history, but in both the lower of itself does not produce the higher. If we were to admit this, we would always find a new factor in the higher for which no casuality was provided in the lower. In order to provide this casuality we posit the divine agency as the only adequate explanation, and charge radical criticism with total inability to provide a naturalistic explanation which is adequate.

In the second place, a careful study of the history set forth in the Scriptures shows that each successive age pre-supposes the preceding age and its contents. This can be made clear even if we grant that there are, as the critics say, two lines of history, the prophetic and the priestly, blended together in the narratives as we now have them. If we begin with the age of Ezra, it can be shown that the incidents which happened in connection with the restoration from the Exile, and the whole scope of what Ezra did, do not mark an onward natural development, but are only possible under the supposition that mature Mosaism existed before that day. If we take our stand at the time of Josiah, or Hezekiah, the proceedings of that age in like manner pre-suppose the reality of the fully-developed Mosaic system, and so do not mark the origin of something entirely new. In like manner, if space permitted, it would be possible, by tracing the history back through the period of the early Kings and the confused era of the Judges, to show that each stage pre-supposed, as already existent, mature Mosaism as the ideal which was ever set before the people. The only way by which this argument can be set aside, is to deny the reality of the history as it now stands ; and, if this be done, there is an end of all debate on the lines of historical investigation and proof.

In the third place, silence regarding the actual observance of the complete ritual and legislation of the Mosaic system does not prove the nonexistence of that system in its mature form. The critics make much of this argument. They tell us again and again, that we have no account of the observance of the Deuteronomic code during the period of the Judges, and no information that the Priestly code was in force during the days of the early Kings. From this silence regarding these things, the critics conclude that these codes did not exist during these periods. Now it can be shown that the critics exaggerate the measure of silence which the history exhibits in regard to this observance or non-observance. And, further, when the critics find that there is what looks like a clear allusion to the existence of mature Mosaism in the earlier history, they boldly shout, "Interpolation," or carry the history forward to the era which suits their theory. This, again, is an end of all debate which rests on an historic basis. And again, it by no means follows that, because legislation and ritual were not observed, then they were not existent and binding, nor should we conclude that because there is no historical statement about their observance, therefore they were not observed by the people. The history itself shows that the people often fell away and came far short of the ideal before them, and there is every reason to believe that through long periods of peace and prosperity the Mosaic system was regularly observed when the history naturally has little to say about it. The history, too, especially during the unsettled period of the judges, gives us, in part, the reasons which would sufficiently account for the imperfect obedience to a system of ritual and legislation which all the while was real and obligatory upon the people.

The argument from silence, moreover, proves far too much. If it proves the non-existence of the Priestly code prior to the Exile, it will also prove its non-existence after the Exile. For the striking fact, often overlooked by the critics, is nevertheless true that we find just as little historical allusion to the mature Mosaic system after the Exile as before it, and especially is it the case that never after the Exile is there any allusion to the Ark of the Testimony with which many of the details of the Priestly code were associated. The argument *a silentio* consequently proves either too little or too much, and may be set aside as of no value for the critics in support of their conclusions.

In the fourth place, according to the critical reconstruction of the history, no proper account can be given of the revolt of the ten tribes, and the consequent division of the people into the two kingdoms, each of which has its separate history.

GENERAL HISTORICAL DEFECTS. 189

As to the historicity of this division, no doubt can be entertained, unless the whole history of the nation be resolved into myth or legend. Admitting the real historical nature of the revolt and subsequent career of the two kingdoms, we find that over three centuries before the days of Josiah, and fully five centuries prior to the time of Ezra, the Mosaic system as represented by the Samaritan Pentateuch must have existed. The reply which the critics make, to the effect that this Pentateuch was not produced till long after the division, does not help the case, even if it had anything in its support. It is scarcely likely that the kingdom of Israel would borrow their complex ritual system from the kingdom of Judah, for there was such an antagonism between them that this would be exceedingly improbable, and to suppose that a similar natural evolution of rite and law took place in Israel as in Judah, and that it was written out in that Pentateuch in later times, is almost out of the question. We press this consideration against the critics, and are free to confess that, though we have read a good deal of the writings of the critics, we cannot recall any satisfactory account of the division of the nation, and of the contents of the Samaritan Pentateuch given by radical criticism.

Moreover, from the history of this division, we cannot fail to note that the Samaritans held to monotheism, and one central sanctuary which they set up for themselves at Mt. Gerizim. This would seem to indicate that the nation was, even at that time, monotheistic, and was directed to hold worship specially at one central sanctuary. It cannot be supposed that the ten tribes were far in advance of the two tribes at that time, and yet the critics tell us that monotheism and worship at one shrine in the kingdom of Judah did not come to be the fact till the days of Josiah and Ezra. Of course, in presenting the historical argument based upon the Samaritan Pentateuch we are aware that the critics have their theory of this form of the Pentateuch which is in harmony with that which they hold regarding its Judaic form. We simply emphasize the fact that radical criticism has to deal with both forms of the Pentateuch, and that this fact renders their problem more complex.

In the fifth place, we wish merely to mention some other general historical matters in the briefest possible way before this chapter closes. First, we charge the critical theory with utterly destroying the historical continuity of the Messianic promise. Taking the history as it stands in Scripture, we find this line of glorious promise running like a golden thread all through the Old Testament history. Adopting the critical reconstructive theory, we defy any person to follow that thread. It is broken, twisted, and reduced to a tangle before our eyes. Secondly, on the critical basis it is impossible to construct the history of Judges, Kings, and Chronicles. The theory destroys the history, and fails to reconstruct it. This period is confessedly difficult, but the conviction ever deepens in our minds that the critical theory increases the difficulties which it presents to the scholar. Thirdly, the method of historical reconstruction which the critics pursue, tends to reduce the history to fiction or myth. If the history be the imaginary filling in of a later age, how does it deserve the name of history? If it be all myth, gradually assuming definite form, the historical basis is destroyed altogether, and the religion of Israel is mythology. If this be the case, Christianity can scarcely be different in its nature. In conclusion, we charge radical criticism with being utterly false and unscientific in its historical methods. Are the critics of the present day likely to be better judges of the real history of those ancient times than those who lived and wrote at or near the period of the events? We only wish that space permitted the expansion of these points which have been merely mentioned.

CHAPTER V.

PARTICULAR HISTORICAL DEFECTS.

IN the last chapter some general historical tests were applied to the radical theory, and by this means it was found to be defective at several important points. In this chapter the historical criticism is continued, and some particular considerations are adduced in connection with the contentions of advanced criticism.

In the first place, we allude to the testimony of Josephus, who lived about the middle of the first century of the Christian era. It is simply saying what all who have read the writings of this literary Jew, know, to remark that his view of the history and religious development of Israel coincides with the biblical theory. The same is true not only of the early Jewish opponents of Christianity, but also of its pagan assailants. Celsus, Porphyry, and Julian agree in the main with Josephus in regard to the history of Israel.

Josephus knows nothing of the modern radical theory, and seems in no degree to feel the need of reconstructing the history of Israel. His historical writings are indeed a commentary on the history of Israel, and of its national and religious life as depicted in the Scriptures. Now, Josephus was in a position to be as well informed as any man upon this subject. Surely he was better able to give an opinion than the critics of to-day, who live eighteen centuries later than he, and cannot possibly have any additional materials in their hands. How came this learned Jew to fall into a great error which remained undiscovered until modern critics found it out? We adduce the testimony of Josephus against the radical reconstructive code theory of the history, legislation, and ritual of Israel, and press the critics for an explanation of the facts in the case at this point.

In the second place, we call special attention to the historical setting of the whole Mosaic religious system, and wish to point out how this tells against the hypothesis of the radical critics in general, especially as to its contention that not until late in the history of Israel, and only by successive codes, did the system reach its complex maturity. Against the critics we contend that the complete legislation has its definite historical setting, according to which it looks back to Egypt and forward to Canaan. The people are out of Egypt, but not yet in Canaan, when the complete religious system is given them. The attempt of the critics to turn the edge of this contention by saying that the history has been thrown back has no sense or propriety in it. It is simply denying history, and rendering historical debate impossible. What would be the sense of describing the people as not yet in Canaan, when as a matter of fact they had been there for centuries? And wherein is the propriety of filling in the history in later times in this peculiar manner, when as a matter of fact the whole is imaginary?

Holding by the historicity of the wilderness experiences and doings, we quote a passage or two, to show that for all the three so-called codes this historical setting — out of Egypt, but not yet in Canaan — holds good. In Ex. 12 : 25, which is part of the literature of the covenant code, we read, "And it shall come to pass when ye be come to the land which the Lord will give you, according as he hath promised, that ye shall keep this service." In Deut. 1 : 8, which is part of the Deuteronomic code, according to the critics, that did not come into existence until the days of Josiah, we read, "Behold, I have set the land before you: go in and possess the land which the Lord sware unto your fathers." Israel is not yet in Canaan. Will the critics rise and explain? Again, Lev. 14 : 34, which constitutes the central part of the Priestly code, and which the critics contend did not appear until about the days of Ezra, makes this remarkable statement: "When ye be come into the land of Canaan, which I give to you for a possession." Israel is not yet in Canaan, in Ezra's day. Will the critics rise and explain? Once more, in Num. 15 : 2, also a part of the literature of the Priestly code, we find this utterance: "When ye be come

PARTICULAR HISTORICAL DEFECTS. 195

into the land of your habitations which I give unto you." Israel is not yet in Canaan. Will the critics venture to explain these and many similar passages?

These are only a tithe of the passages which might be quoted indiscriminately from the literature of all the so-called codes, to show that when the complete Mosaic ritual and legal system was given, Israel was out of Egypt but not yet in Canaan. This tells with fatal effect against the notion of the three codes, different in contents, and far apart in time. It also tells against the opinion of the critics that the Mosaic system was a slow evolutionary product, only complete long after the people were in Canaan. The reply of the critics, to the effect that those historical allusions are not to be literally understood, we submit, is no answer at all. To say that these references to historical facts are merely the filling in of the story, or are interpolations, is simply to shirk the question, and make no reply. We therefore press the critics for an explanation of the well-defined historical setting of the complete Mosaic system. Till this on solid historical grounds is given, we shall hold still to the old biblical view.

In the third place, the natural historical explanation of the reform under Josiah, and of the restoration under Ezra is far more reasonable than the hypotheses of the advanced critics. We have already seen that radical criticism makes very much of these crises in the history of Israel. In connection with both, an onward impulse was given to the religion of Israel, and the Deuteronomic and Priestly codes then came into existence. Against all the elaborate reasoning and baseless speculation of the critics upon the events of these two great eras in the career of Israel, we maintain that the far more natural and simple view is to regard them to be what the terms "reform" and "restoration" signify.

Instead of the reform in Josiah's day being a new religious era marked by the genesis of the Deuteronomic code, it was simply a *reform* which led the people from idolatry back to the old paths of the religion of their fathers, which was contained in the "law given by Moses," and which embraced in its contents the entire system with its so-called three codes. To take any other view, raises needless and endless difficulties. How can we reconcile with sound morality the supposition of the critics, to the effect that Hilkiah and others drew up the book, brought it to the king and pretended that it was found in the Temple? Then how came the king to be so deeply affected, if the document was merely a *reform programme*, and not the old law under which he knew that his fathers lived and prospered? And, again, how could Hilkiah and the king foist upon the people something so entirely new, without calling forth their opposition? It could scarcely be, even during the sixty years of idolatry in the reigns of the father and grandfather of Josiah, that all knowledge of the old law and its prescriptions had died out. If it had, the difficulty of bringing in an entirely new order of things would be very great; yet no such difficulty appears on the part of the people. If there still remained some true, devout souls, then the bringing forth of the book and the institution of the reform according to its prescriptions would meet their approval. But to impose a new scheme upon such people would be almost sure to arouse opposition. The biblical view has the merit of being the simple and natural one, while the critical theory is burdened with difficulties from which it can afford no relief.

So in reference to the restoration from the Exile in the dark days of Ezra. That Ezra and others produced during the Exile the elaborate Priestly code is an assumption for which no good proof is adduced. That the contents of that code did *not* exist prior to the Exile is not proved by the critics. The carrying away of the furniture and vessels of the Temple would seem to indicate that the ritual with which these things were associated was actually in force before the Exile. Then the whole history of the restoration looks as if the people were returning to the old order of things, which had been interrupted for the seventy years of exile. Indeed, a strong case might, in our judgment, be made out for the view that had the completed Mosaic ritual and legislation not existed prior to the Exile, it could not have been brought to its maturity during that dark era ; and that, unless we presuppose the completed system of law and ritual, the restoration itself would scarcely have been possible. The critics can only give plausibility to their theories by treating these periods unnaturally, and by virtually ignoring plain, simple, historical narratives. But this is surely uncritical criticism !

In the fourth place, there are several clear historical facts which tell with much force against the radical explanation of the history of the Old Testament. There are many of these which might be adduced, but we select only two as samples of the rest, and as showing how very unhistorical radical criticism actually becomes.

The first case has reference to the choice of a king by Israel. This is found in Deut. 17 : 14-20, a passage too long to quote here, but which we advise our readers to look into carefully. Here we have the directions given, before the people have entered Canaan, as to the choice of a king in after days, and advice set down for the guidance of the king. Now, mark that, according to the critics, this passage stands in the Deuteronomic code which they further tell us did not exist or come into force till near the time of Josiah, at least eight centuries after the people had been at Sinai. The absurdity is evident, unless we allow the critics to turn the history upside down. What would be the sense in giving rules about the selection of a king, and of telling the king what manner of man he should be, when the people already had had kings for three or four centuries? We wait patiently for the critics' answer.

The second illustration of the inversion of history, of which radical criticism is guilty, is in reference to the destruction of the Amalekites. In Deut. 25: 19, we have the command "to blot out the remembrance of Amalek from under heaven." Then in 1 Sam. 30, we have an account of the utter destruction of Amalek in the days of David. Now, mark again, that the command to blot out Amalek was given in what is part of the Deuteronomic code, which the critics place near Josiah's time, and the command has been completely fulfilled in the days of David, over three centuries before the age of Josiah. What would be the sense of giving a command to destroy a people, when the people in question did not exist? We await the answer of the critics here with patience.

We are aware of the attempts made by the radical critics to turn the edge of such sharp criticism as these particular historic facts make of their theory. We know how they attempt to juggle with history, and turn chronology upside down. Ruled by the terms of their own theories, they do not hesitate to rule out history altogether, and reconstruct the history or allege interpolation. Rejecting the natural biblical views of the religion and history of Israel on account of their supposed difficulties, they give us schemes which are far more complicated, and require greater faith to accept. And, further, they overlook the fact that the reality of the history is always presupposed by the Psalms and Prophecy of later days. In these, the history itself is often recounted in a way which is totally inexplicable on the critical basis. We hesitate not to charge radical criticism with being unhistorical while professing to be historical, and with being uncritical while claiming to be highly critical, and, above all, with giving us an ill-constructed scheme in which difficulties are made or magnified, and faith in the Scriptures placed under a severer strain than it can possibly be by the biblical theory.

CHAPTER VI.

THE DOCUMENTARY HYPOTHESIS.

Two chapters have been devoted to criticism of the philosophical aspects of radical theories of the religion of the sacred Scriptures, and two have dealt with some historical lines of examination bearing upon the soundness of these theories. We found in these chapters that the philosophy involved was defective, and that the radical theories of the critics would not stand the test of historical inquiry.

With this chapter we enter upon other lines of examination, and take up, first of all, the *documentary hypothesis*. We shall look at this hypothesis on its own merits, and consider also the use which radical criticism makes of this hypothesis in its support. In general, the critics maintain that the Old Testament books were not produced by single authors, but are composite productions, resulting from the work of compiling and recasting by successive hands, documents of various kinds which already existed. On a large scale, therefore, the documentary hypothesis is pressed into the service of the reconstructive theories. Into this feature of radical criticism this chapter makes inquiry.

In the first place, we beg to remind our readers of the source whence this hypothesis at first emerged, and of the use then made of it. In the history of radical criticism given in the opening chapters of this book, it was pointed out that we owe the documentary hypothesis in its complete form to Astruc, a physician at Paris. Whether he intended it or not, we find, and that without any protest from him, that this documentary scheme was used by infidelity to break down the integrity of the Scriptures, and to greatly lessen their divine authority by giving undue prominence to the human element in them. So we see that this hypothesis was born outside the Church, and for a time was the open foe of revealed religion. In our judgment, it still is, if not a secret enemy, at least a dangerous ally of evangelical views of revealed truth.

In the second place, we take the position that advanced criticism makes far too much of the notion of various documents which are supposed to have been used very extensively by the authors of the sacred books. We are not concerned to deny that in some cases the authors of the sacred Scriptures may, under the guidance of the Holy Spirit, have used pre-existing writings or documents. This is possible, in our judgment, in the case of some of the writings of Moses. In the case of the books of

Kings and Chronicles, it is much more likely that their author, or authors, used previously existing documents. So perhaps in the Psalter we have there some sacred songs which were already extant, as we find some of these psalms, in substance, in the historical books. But what we contend for against radical criticism is the position that it makes far too much of the documentary hypothesis, and that it pushes what, at best, is an unproved assumption, to an extreme which cannot be justified by the facts in the case. We wish that we had space to illustrate the method of the critics at this point. The reader will recall the symbols "J," "E," "JE," "D," "P," and "R," each of which represents a different series of documents, which, together, were finally wrought up into a composite whole. In this way, and in an almost entirely naturalistic manner, the Scriptures grew and grew till they reached their final stage. We here charge radical criticism with laying far too much stress on this hypothesis, and we simply demand proof clear and complete that such documents existed, and that they were used as largely by the authors of the various books of the Bible, as the critics supposed they were. Will the critics give the proof?

In the third place, we take a step further, and allege that the procedure of the critics at this point is entirely superficial. It busies itself with the literary form of the Scriptures, and reaches conclusions, not by presenting external proof but by the exercise of subjective opinions. Perhaps we can do nothing better here than to give an illustration or two taken from Driver, who, though largely a follower of Dillmann, cannot by any means be called an extremely radical critic, for he does not professedly discard belief in the supernatural. Let the reader open his Bible at Genesis 37, where the story of Joseph begins, and follow the analysis of Driver. From the middle of verse 2 to the end of verse 11 belongs to the document " E," then from verse 12 to verse 21, we have an extract from the writing known as " J." From verse 22 to verse 24, " E " comes in again, to be followed by verses 25-27 from " J." Then will the reader specially note the documentary analysis of verse 28. From the beginning of the verse down to the word "pit," we have " E ; " from "pit" down to "silver," " J " comes in ; then from "silver" to the end of the verse, we are assured that " E " is the source, as also it is of the passage on to the close of verse 30. To complete the analysis of the chapter, verses 31-35 are taken from " J," and verse 36 reverts again to " E."

For another example, take the first two chapters of Exodus. Here 1 : 1-7 comes from "P ; " 1 : 8-12 from " E ; " 1 : 13, 14 from "P ; " 1 : 15-22 from " E " again. So, also, 2 : 1-23 to the word "died," in verse 23, is due to " E," and from "died" to the end of the chapter we find " P " again the source. As a concluding example, let the reader turn to Joshua 5-8, where Driver gives the

THE DOCUMENTARY HYPOTHESIS. 205

following analysis: Here 5:1 belongs to a document known as "D_2," verses 2, 3 to "J E," and verses 4-7 come again from "D_2," while verses 8, 9 are from "J E." Then "P" appears, giving us verses 10-12, followed again by "J E," who completes chapter 5, and gives us the whole of chapter 6. For chapter 7 "P" gives us verse 1; "J E" verses 2-26. "J E" also provides us with chapter 8: 1-29, and "D_2" turns up to give us verses 30-35 of this chapter.

These illustrations will suffice to exhibit the documentary methods of even moderate critics, and at the same time will go far to justify the charge we are now making against radical criticism, to the effect that it is entirely superficial. It might very properly be added that it is also entirely artificial. Could anything be more artificial than the manner in which Gen. 37:28 is analyzed. It is cut into three fragments, two of which come from "E," and one in the middle of the verse comes from "J." Then, too, we may not forget that the critics are not at all agreed as to the precise way in which the analysis of passages should be made. If we had space to compare half a dozen critics on any single passage, we would see more fully how superficial and artificial the whole procedure is. Each critic is a law unto himself, and when we seek to gather up "the assured results of modern scholarship," we find no results in which the majority of the critics are agreed. We believe that conservative criticism has a splendid campaign before it at this point in the controversy if it will simply follow step by step the tracks of the critics, and show how superficial their work must of necessity be at every step.

In the fourth place, we take the ground against radical criticism that, even if the Scriptures were composed after the manner which the critics allege, the proof of that fact cannot now be adduced. The critics can at this day only suppose the existence of these various documents. They cannot tell us who their authors were, and what the circumstances of their production. They only assume their existence, label these hypothetical documents with certain symbols and proceed with their critical processes. The Scriptures afford no clear proof of the existence, on such a large scale, of extant documents, and still less is there proof that the authors of the sacred books used them in such a wholesale way as the critics assert. Now, surely the conservative critics are not to be blamed for declining to join the radicals, at least until the latter give some reasonable proof for all they say about the documentary composition of the sacred Scriptures. Mere suppositions are not enough, nor will the unsupported opinion of a critic, no matter how boldly expressed, carry much weight until the reliable historical evidence is forthcoming. This proof, we assert, is not presented by the critics, and from the nature of the case most of the evidence does not now exist. How absurd the claims of the critics really are, and how unlikely that their views shall permanently prevail! The whole procedure is far more like a product of the imagination than the result of sober criticism.

In the fifth place, reasons can so far be given for the use of the divine names Jehovah and Elohim, without assuming distinct documents and different authors of these documents. We have already seen that the first hint of the documentary hypothesis was given to Astruc from the way in which these divine names were found in Genesis. Finding these names used separately and conjointly in certain passages, the conclusion was reached that there must have been separate documents from which the compiler of Genesis drew his materials. The hint thus given was by other writers extended to the whole Pentateuch at least, and the existence and use of a great many documents was assumed by the critics. Now against this view it can be shown, with a good deal of certainty, that these names denote different aspects of the Divine Being, and that the name of the Almighty which occurs in any special passage agrees with the general subject matter of that passage. Hence, in the first chapter of Genesis we naturally expect Elohim, which denotes God as natural Creator, and in the second chapter we find Jehovah-Elohim, and see the propriety of this in the fact that besides the notion of Creator, the fact of revelation appears. So in the twelfth chapter, when the covenant is made with Abraham, the name Jehovah alone properly appears. In this consistent usage of these names we have a natural explanation of the facts of which the documentary hypothesis gives us at best but a clumsy explanation, and one which when pushed to its critical extreme is simply absurd. The hypothesis, therefore, is needless.

In the last place, the literary analysis of the documentary hypothesis, as proposed by radical critics, threatens to destroy the wonderful organic unity of the Scriptures. The fact of this unity has always been noticed. This very remarkable collection of writings, made by men of different ages, lands, and literary ability, has yet a most remarkable unity, which can be properly described by no other term than the word *organic*. Now we maintain against the critics that the literary dissection made by them threatens the organic life of the volume. Their procedure is as if a living body were placed on the table, and the lance of dissection applied to it. If the dissection be carried out, the life of the body is destroyed, and a corpse is the result. So with the radical critics and their literary methods as now before us. They take the Scriptures as a living organic unit, subject them to the dismemberment of the lance of literary criticism, and the result is that the unity is broken, and the organic life is destroyed. In this way, one of the chief proofs of the divinity and inspiration of the book is destroyed, and it is virtually killed by the critics so far as it is the living word of God. We charge radical criticism with *literary vivisection*, so cruel that it theatens to destroy the organic divine life of the sacred Scriptures. The next chapter deals with the postulate of the three codes which is closely related to the documentary hypothesis.

CHAPTER VII.

THE THREE CODES.

CLOSELY connected with the documentary hypothesis in the radical theory is the supposition of *three distinct legal and ritual codes* in the completed Mosaic system. This chapter proceeds to examine this supposition, which in various forms is an essential part of the radical schemes. In brief, as already explained in a former chapter, the hypothesis of the three codes presents the view that in mature Mosaism, as set forth in the early books of the Old Testament Scriptures, there are three distinct and different ritual and legal schemes which are diverse at several essential points, and which came into existence and observance at long intervals of time from each other. These are called the Covenant, the Deuteronomic, and the Priestly codes, respectively. This position of radical criticism at this point is to be examined in this chapter with some care.

In the first place, we raise the question whether there are or ever were really three codes, different in their contents and belonging to ages widely apart from each other in time. Have the critics not assumed the three codes without good grounds? Has

THE THREE CODES. 211

radical criticism produced sufficient proof of its supposition concerning the codes? Are there such radical differences between these three so-called codes as to necessitate a distinctive origin for each? And do the critics give satisfactory reasons for assuming that the three codes came successively into existence with several centuries intervening between them?

Much that has already been said in the chapter upon the historical defects of the radical theory, and upon the weakness of the documentary hypothesis, has force under this head. The critics actually make such an analysis of the literature as necessitates codification of the ritual, whereas if the natural historical view of the literature be taken, there will be no necessity for assuming the diverse and successive codes at all. Here again we call upon the critics to give us the proof of the assertion that there are, or ever were, three distinct codes of law and ritual in force in Israel at different periods of its history. As proof we ask for something more than the opinion of the critic; we demand the historical evidence which a matter of fact like this always should have for its support. Instead of interpreting the history in the light of three codes, we demand proof from the history to justify the assumption that there are three codes.

In the second place, it may be shown that the so-called three codes, instead of being diverse and successive, so involve each other that they must be held to be a unit and contemporaneous. To work this point out fully would require more space than we have at our command in this series of chapters. It would require a careful comparison, not only of the points of difference in the codes upon which the radical critics lay so much stress, but a comparison of those resemblances which are of such a nature as to show that the codes involve each other. Is it not reasonable to suppose that the contents of the Covenant code were given first in order, and then, as the history of what took place at Sinai shows, the elaboration of what the critics call the Priest's code immediately followed? And, after the wilderness wandering was over, as the history again suggests, we find that the so-called Deuteronomic code was given, chiefly as a summary of the other codes, but partly also embracing some new laws; and the whole was given complete as a complex unit before the people entered Canaan at all. It clearly rests upon the radical critics to show that this is not the true state of the case. To assume the evolutionary theory of the development of the religion of Israel, which has been already criticised, and then to assume that the three codes must have come into existence in the order of their complexity, and during a period of several centuries, is not to adduce proof of the existence and differences in these assumed codes. We demand the proof.

This proof we have already found wanting, and so now we set aside the reasoning based on it in support of the hypothesis of the three codes in the Mosaic system. As in the doctrine of the Trinity, we have three persons in one essence, not three Deities, so in the religion of Israel we have three phases or stages of one divinely originated system of ritual and legislation, which so involve each other as to be incapable of actual separation, and which together constituted the ideal according to which the whole subsequent religious life and activity of Israel were to be framed. That they came short of this ideal many a time may be the sad fact, but this shortcoming by no means proves the non-existence of the ideal from the beginning.

In the third place, we point out the fact that the radical critics are not at all agreed as to the *order* of succession in which the three codes came into existence. The strict Wellhausen school argue that the order is : Covenant code, Deuteronomic code, Priestly code. The first originated about the time of Moses ; the second near the days of Josiah ; the third sprang up at the era of the Exile. But there is a very influential school of critics represented by writers like Schrader, Dillmann, and others, who give the order to be : Covenant, Priestly, and Deuteronomic codes. This view is fatal to the Wellhausen contention concerning the order of the codes as represented by English speaking critics like Driver and Cheyne. In this connection it is interesting to notice the fact that Klostermann, professor of Old Testament Exegesis in the University of Kiel, is recently out in a series of effective philippics against the extravagant results and indefensible critical methods of the Wellhausen School. Then, too, there is no sufficient agreement among the critics as to what elements of the complete Mosaic system are to be assigned to each code, nor as to the precise relations which subsist among the various strata of legislation which together make up mature Mosaism. So long as the critics continue to wage civil war among themselves, we need not be disturbed. We may wait with patience till the critics settle at least their main positions. The contention of Dillmann that the Deuteronomic code is last in order, is certainly a concession to the views of conservative criticism, and the onslaught of Klostermann upon the main positions of the Wellhausen school, should certainly call a halt on the part of Anglo-Saxon critics, many of whom seem to have gone over, bag and baggage, to the Wellhausen camp. Perhaps we shall find after all, when the din of critical warfare has ceased, that "the assured results of modern scholarship" are not so fully assured as was claimed, and that the conservative critics are not only in full possession of the field but more firmly entrenched there than ever before.

THE THREE CODES. 215

In the fourth place, assuming the historicity of the Old Testament narratives, it is possible to trace the existence of the Priest's code back from the days of Ezra, and of the Deuteronomic code back from the time of Josiah to the period of the conquest of Canaan. This, again, is a position the proof of which cannot be exhibited at length in our present limits, but we believe that it presents a most effective line of criticism upon the hypothesis of the three codes, and so upon the very citadel of the radical critical theory. If the conservative critics begin with mature Mosaism at the time of Ezra, and by means of the historical allusions to the contents of the Priest's code found in the historical books, and also, by means of the writings of the prophets, are able to trace the Priest's code at least to a period prior to the date when the critics assert that the Deuteronomic code came into existence, and when, of course, only the Covenant code existed, they have successfully assailed the critical theory of the three codes. This we firmly believe conservative criticism can do. Indeed, it has done so already in general terms, but the door is open for the conservatives to do still more effective work along this pathway then even Robertson, in his "Early Religion of Israel," has so ably done in the limits at his disposal in that treatise. Recent articles by Dr. W. Henry Green, of Princeton, are of much value in this connection.

The evasions of the critics, which they attempt to make again and again, to ward off the force of this line of criticism, by denying the real historicity of the narratives accompanying the codes, is either unjustifiable, or suicidal. It is unjustifiable we fully believe, and utterly rash and foolhardy to juggle thus with the history under the intoxicating effects of a theory. But even if the critical treatment of the history be admitted as valid, we charge it with being suicidal, for the same reasoning which reduces the history to fiction or myth, will also reduce the contents of the codes to the same category. Then assuredly the religion of Israel becomes mythology, and the historic basis of Christianity is forever destroyed.

In the last place, we beg the radical critics to tell us how it came to pass that the people of Israel in successive ages, as the several codes came into existence, and the literature exhibiting them took its form, always attributed the whole to Moses and his age. In some way the people were led to believe that by him the laws of the several codes were enacted, by him the ritual of the codes in order was prescribed, and by him even most of the literature was put into definite shape. We ask for an explanation of these facts on the critical basis. It is evident that the name of Moses carried very great weight, and, we ask, how did it acquire all this authority, unless he had had far more to do with the genesis of the religion of Israel than the radical theory allows? Passing by altogether the difficulty of *literary imposture*, which the critics are bound to face here, surely the natural explanation of the facts is that Moses was the medium by whom the complete system bearing his name was given by Jehovah to the people, and that to his hand we owe the main body of the writings which contain that system. This is the simple, natural view to which we believe that we may still adhere, while the critical theory of the codes is unnatural and hampered by endless difficulties. When will the critics be content with simplicity and naturalness?

CHAPTER VIII.

DEUTERONOMY.

HAVING in the last chapter made a brief examination of the hypothesis of the three codes, and having found that it was open to criticism at several vulnerable points, we proceed in this chapter to consider in a more definite way the book of Deuteronomy, and to determine the place it really holds in the Mosaic system.

The topic to be thus considered in this chapter is one of cardinal importance in the controversy between conservative and radical criticism. How is the book of Deuteronomy and the scheme of law and ritual which it represents to be understood? Is it the second stage in the development of the Mosaic system, which was the product of natural evolution of religion among the people of Israel, or is it a summary and recapitulation, with some slight additions, of the Mosaic legislation made by Moses on the eve of their entry into Canaan? Radical criticism in a general way takes the former view; and yet not with entire uniformity, as we have already seen. Then even these radical critics who hold, as the Wellhausen school does, that Deuternomic legislation only came into existence in

Josiah's day, are by no means agreed as to the precise mode by which it came into existence. Some are inclined to the view that it came suddenly into existence as a program of reform; others prefer to hold that the legislation previously existed among the people as an oral code, and was reduced to written codified form shortly before the days of Josiah.

Then as to the relation between Deuteronomy and its code and the Covenant code of the Jehovistic documents, the critics have not yet reached harmony of opinion. How much of the Covenant code is implied in the Deuteronomic, how far monotheism is due to the Deuteronomic code, and to what extent the Covenant code prescribed worship only at one central sanctuary, are questions upon which criticism of the radical type has not yet given us its "assured results." To press this lack of agreement against radical criticism at this point is really a complete refutation of its contentions concerning the book of Deuteronomy, so that we might arrest our critique with having pointed out this fact. Still we may carry the war into Africa against radical criticism, and in this chapter we propose to examine some of its reasonings connected with the problem presented by Deuteronomy.

In the first place, assuming the real historical nature of the narratives contained in the book of Deuteronomy, we claim that the natural view to take of it is that it is Mosaic, in the sense at least that it belongs to the age of Moses and took its complete form at least prior to the conquest of Canaan under Joshua. The contents of the first chapter sound the historic keynote at this point. The repetition of the decalogue was the most natural thing in the circumstances, and the presentation of the promises and the threatenings at the close of the book was entirely suitable to the status of the people when they were just about to enter the land of promise. We ask the critics to show any sort of plausibility in having these promises and threatenings made after the people had been in the land for centuries, as their theory implies.

The contention of the critics at this point that the ritual code did not exist at the time of the Conquest, but that the history to which we have alluded was written up in later times, and was projected back to fill up the narrative, is idle and absurd. We are getting tired of this absurd contention. If the history though written later records the real process of events, then it is real history, and it carries the code with it. The only escape from this conclusion is by attempting the impossible feat of separating the history and the ritual. If, on the other hand, the professed narratives are fictitious, then there is an end of debate, and the whole is a work of ingenious fiction.

In the second place, those laws which the critics say are peculiar to Deuteronomy are just such as we would expect to be given prior to the entrance of the people into Canaan. Then, further, there are laws which could have meaning to the people only in prospect of setting their feet in Canaan, as, for example, the division of the land among the tribes, and the regulations regarding landmarks. Then the strong words and severe punishment announced regarding idolatry are most fitting, just as the people are about to come into contact with the Canaanites who are wholly given to idolatry. Moreover, these laws regarding idolatry are but an expansion and application of the first and second commands of the ten words, made at a most fitting time. So in like manner, the regulations regarding the cities of refuge have their natural explanation from the time of the Conquest rather than from the days of Josiah. Then, too, the laws regarding rulers and officers found in Deuteronomy, especially the regulations concerning the choice of a king, are in their natural place on the eve of the establishment of the national life of the people in their own land. So all through the book we could go, making references which go to show that the legislation it contains fits the period of Moses and the Conquest far best; and it would be made plain that to place it at the era of Josiah would render much of it obsolete or meaningless. Conservative criticism has a strong case at this point, and should follow it out.

In the third place, the account which the critics give of the absence of ritual regulations in Deuteronomy is by no means adequate, and can only be regarded as the product of a preconceived theory. We are told by the radical critics that the elaborate ritual of the Priestly code did not exist, since in the history of this period there are few references to it, and in Deuteronomy there is very little allusion to the elaborate details of the Levitical system. Hence, we are told that these details did not yet exist. The reader will at once perceive that this is really the argument *a silentio* to which allusion was made in a previous chapter. It either proves nothing, or else it proves too much, as was then shown. Consequently, it does not follow that because there is little allusion to elaborate sacrifice and to the great annual feasts, therefore these things were not existent and obligatory. Even non-observance would not prove their non-existence, and so we see again that all this sort of reasoning is utterly unworthy the name of sober criticism. But further, the code which was in force in connection with the elaborate Temple service could only be the Deuteronomic, for, according to the radical critics, the Priestly code did not exist till about the time of the Exile. And yet the critics tell us that this very code, being barren of frequent allusions to ritual details, proves that there was no elaborate ritual in existence. Surely the far more natural view is to hold that the complete Mosaic system was in existence, and observed more or less carefully from the first, and that as matters moved on in the even tenor of their way, there was no reason to be constantly emphasizing the details of the system, or giving annual accounts of its observance. The absurdity of the critical view is made all the more evident when we add to what has just been said, the fact that in originating the Priestly code at, or after, the Exile, with Ezekiel as the transition between the Deuteronomic and Priestly codes, the critics are really preparing an elaborate code for a Temple all in ruins, for the first temple was destroyed at the beginning of the great captivity.

In the fourth place, the contention of the critics that in Deuteronomy we first find insistence on worship at one central sanctuary is not well founded. The spirit of the Covenant code as represented by the ten words is monotheistic, and looks to a central sanctuary. During the wilderness experience, and in the unsettled state of the nation throughout the period of the Judges, it may have been that this central place was a moveable one, but where the Ark and Tabernacle were, there was the place whither the people were to repair. Then, too, we challenge the critics to prove that previous to the appearance of the Deuteronomic code in the days of Josiah, as they say, idolatry was tolerated by any code, or that worship at a multiplicity of shrines was enjoined. Neither the contents of the Covenant code nor the history of the period in the Jehovistic literature affords any shadow of proof for the critical opinion on this point.

In the fifth place, several other points, did space permit, could be dwelt upon to show how untenable the radical view is on the topic now under notice. The wonderful unity of Deuteronomy, as is well shown even by Dillmann and Delitzsch, tells against the critics. The difficulty of smuggling in the book and its code at the time of Josiah with no protest from the people is a serious matter for the critics to account for. The serious difficulty of providing an author who is as likely as Moses, is one which we may press against the critics; and if he be not the author of the legislation why has it his name? In a word, the critics are bound to prove the non-Mosaic genesis of Deuteronomy before they can establish their case. This they have not yet succeeded in doing.

The critics are also bound to explain the difference between the attitude of Deuteronomy toward Egypt and Edom, and the attitude of Hosea the prophet, who lived just about the time the critics tell us that the Deuteronomic code was taking definite shape as a *praxis* among the people, toward these nations. The prophet and the Deuteronomist are in conflict, according to the critical theory, while according to the conservative view there is no such conflict. Will the critics kindly explain?

In the last place, we believe that the existence of the main contents of Deuteronomy can be traced back from the days of Josiah to the period of the Conquest. This important task is effected by comparing the contents of Deuteronomy with Kings and Chronicles at certain important junctures. The result of that comparison will appear to be that the allusions in the historical books are possible only under the assumption that the contents of Deuteronomy already existed when the history of Kings and Chronicles was drawn up. Compare 2 Kings 14:5, 6 with Deut. 24:16; also 2 Kings 11:12 with Deut. 31:26, and also 2 Chron. 20:10 with Deut. 2:4-19, for examples of what we mean. We are sure that this is a rich mine which conservative criticism will do well to work up fully. The outcome of this work will assuredly be to show that if any reliance is to be placed on the historical books, Deuteronomy existed long before the time the critics assign for its origin. But enough, we trust, has been said to show that the critical view of the book and code of Deuteronomy cannot be successfully maintained. The next chapter will deal with the *graded priesthood*.

CHAPTER IX.

THE GRADED PRIESTHOOD.

THE last chapter discussed the book of Deuteronomy in its relations to the radical theory. It was found that the place and scope of this book, with its ritual and legislation, is incapable of proper explanation on the basis of the radical critical theory. The views of conservative criticism regarding Deuteronomy were also shown to be much more natural and complete; and, consequently, radical criticism has not yet made out a case against these views.

This chapter takes up a somewhat different topic, of which the radical critics make a good deal. That topic is what may be called *the graded priesthood*. The question raised relates to the time and manner in which these grades or orders in the priesthood of the religion of Israel arose. Dominated by the principle of natural evolution, radical criticism holds that at first there were no such grades or orders in the priesthood as are denoted by the terms High Priest, Priests, and Levites, but that this gradation was a development of later times, and only to be found complete and definite in the Priests' code about the time of the

THE GRADED PRIESTHOOD. 227

Exile. We now proceed to examine this contention, and to discover what truth, if any, there is in it. Now, if it can be shown that the graded priesthood actually existed from the beginning of the national and religious life of Israel ; if it can be made plain that from the time of the conquest, High Priests, Priests, and Levites, all ministered in their appointed places, then radical criticism has its claim seriously weakened. In this chapter an attempt will be made to show how this may be done. Of course, in the space at our disposal, only a few hints can be given as to the lines which conservative criticism is to follow in its refutation of radical criticism at this point.

Our first position is that we find the threefold distinction in the priesthood set forth in the book of Deuteronomy. Here we have Priests and Levites often mentioned, and, of course, the existence of the High Priest is uniformly assumed by the author of this book. We have space only to allude to a few passages. In the first verse of the eighteenth chapter we read, "The priests, the Levites, and all the tribe of Levi." The radical critics, of course, contend that this passage does not imply a graded priesthood, and a great deal has been written by them upon the proper construction of the grammar of this passage. We are inclined to think that what follows in the same chapter settles the debate in favor of those who hold that we have here at least a distinction between priests and Levites. For the third verse tells what the priest's due is to be, and verses 6-8 tell us how the Levites are to be provided for. That the High Priest existed at this time may be assumed, from the nature of the case and from the history which is to be considered under another head.

In the 5th verse of the 21st chapter we have the expression: "The priests, the sons of Levi." In chapter 26, verses 3, 4, we find the phrase: "The priest that is in those days." Then in verses 12, 13, of the same chapter, we have the Levite alone mentioned. Such passages clearly mark a distinction between the priests and the Levites, though all were of the tribe of Levi.

In chapter 27, verse 9, we have "Moses and the priests, the Levites" spoken of. Here the Levites are commanded to speak to the people by Moses. Again in the 9th verse of the 31st chapter we read that "Moses wrote this law, and delivered it unto the priests the sons of Levi, which bear the ark of the covenant of the Lord."

From these passages, the natural inference is that at the time of the Deuteronomist, even if we take the critical view that this was about the time of Josiah, we find that the graded priesthood had assumed definite form. We are well aware of the various evasions of the critics at this difficult point, yet we are inclined to think that these evasions only make the problem more difficult, and so afford no relief, and consequently we are justified in still maintaining the conservative views.

In the second place, special provision was made from the beginning for the support of the tribe of Levi, and priests and Levites were each to have their particular means of sustenance. This tribe was given no definite inheritance in the land, but certain cities in it were set apart for their occupancy. And from the sacrifices certain portions were to be given to the priests and Levites, and the tithes in part were for the same purpose. Another thing is important here. As one reads the regulations about the priests and Levites and concerning their support in Deuteronomy, the implication often seems to be made that another complete system of rules such as is found in Numbers and Leviticus, already existed. It is only on this supposition that some passages seem to be intelligible. This, if the case, would presuppose the existence of the Priest's code prior to that of Deuteronomy ; and the force of this would lead to the conclusion that mature Mosaism, including the graded priesthood, existed among the people from the conquest. This assumption, we are sure, explains the limited references in Deuteronomy to details of priesthood and ritual much more naturally than the hypothesis of non-existence, when there is little or no allusion to this matter in the writings in question.

In the third place, in the historical books, we find frequent references to certain well defined distinctions in the Levitical orders. In Joshua and Judges, as well as in the later historical books giving us an account of the condition of things in the days of the early kings, we find these references. The existence of the High Priest from the first is undoubted. Aaron stands first in order, and the account of his installation must be regarded as historical, and not a fiction of Ezra's time when the Priests' code is supposed to have arisen. He, according to Deut. 10:6, was succeeded by Eleazar, his son, in the priest's office. Then, in Joshua 14:1, we find this same Eleazar side by side with Joshua distributing the land among the tribes after the conquest. In the last verse of the last chapter of Joshua, we find that Eleazar was succeeded by his son Phinehas. Then the links are wanting, but we find Eli later on, and Abiathar and Zadok and others mentioned, which would indicate the existence of the line of succession more or less definitely.

In like manner if we follow out the historical books, we shall find that the priests and the Levites are often mentioned. In Joshua, in crossing the Jordan, the priests bore the ark, and in the capture of Jericho the priests marched around the city. In Joshua 21:1–8, we have the habitations of the Levites described. The first verse reads thus: "Then came near the heads of the fathers of the Levites unto Eleazar the priest, and unto Joshua the son of Nun." Then follows the account of the homes of the sons of Aaron in order as Levites. Indeed this whole chapter should be read in this connection. In short, the historicity of the books of Joshua and Judges must be impugned, or else we are bound to admit that the graded priesthood was a fact at the time of the Conquest. Hence the frantic effort of the radical critics to get rid of the verdict of this history against their theories is readily understood in view of this consideration. To follow out this line fully is a very important task for conservative criticism to perform.

In the fourth place, if the Tabernacle existed, as we shall show in a subsequent chapter it did, and if the elaborate sacrificial system was in vogue, as we have shown, and shall yet show more fully that it was, then this carries with it the existence of the graded priesthood. And this for the simple reason that for the administration of this completed system, the services of the High Priest, the Priests, and the Levites were all needed. To have an elaborate ritual without the officers to administer it, is unnatural and absurd. From the history of the books of Joshua and Judges, we could again make good this position, and show that the religious system then in vogue needed, as the history also states that it had, a graded priesthood. As this point comes up in another chapter, and for a different purpose, we need add nothing more at this stage.

In the fifth place, the contention of the radical critics that any of the Levites at first could officiate as priests, and that it was only by degrees that the idea of three grades or orders arose, is entirely unfounded. To say, as some of the Wellhausen School do, that there was no High Priest till later times, is to go in the face of the history of the books themselves. To satisfy us that any priest could step in and at his own pleasure act as priest, certainly needs much more proof than has yet been given for it. And, further, what has been already said in reference to the separation of these orders from the first, and the separate provision for their support, all tells against the critics' contention, so that this, too, may be set aside. The case of the Danite, who took a Levite and made him his priest, proves nothing to the point in favor of the critical view, for this strange proceeding was irregular, and arose in a period when the nation was in a disturbed condition. If it means anything, it means that certain distinctions between the Levites already existed.

In the last place, we emphasize the familiar point that the radical view regarding a graded priesthood and the way in which it developed in Israel, is the product of the evolutionary principle which is applied to this particular topic. According to this principle, the simple is first, and the complex last, in the order of development. Here there was a simple condition without gradation at all at first, but by degrees the differentiation took place and the complex graded priesthood was produced. In previous chapters, the inadequacy of this principle to explain the main factors in the religion of Israel was pointed out. We simply fall back on these discussions to make effective our criticism at this point.

Again and again we have seen that the simple historical view of the history and religion of Israel is the natural one. Theories, not facts, rule in the methods of the radical critics. There is a solemn propriety in the fact that some of the radical critics have in recent years been writing articles and making eloquent addresses in which they exalt the use of the imagination in Higher Criticism. Judging from what we have seen in our critique even thus far, the radical critics certainly do exercise the imagination more than the understanding, and the fancy is far more frequently brought into play than the judgment.

CHAPTER X.

THE TABERNACLE.

WE now pass from the priesthood to the *Tabernacle* and the *Ark*. In doing so we come to a very interesting topic in itself considered, and to one concerning which radical criticism has a good deal to say. Moreover, this criticism finds the Tabernacle and its services a rather hard problem to solve. As a matter of fact it supplies a definite concrete object and a fully developed ritual which must puzzle even the imagination of the critics.

If it can be shown that the Tabernacle and its service actually existed from the early stages of the religious history of Israel, radical criticism is virtually refuted at an exceedingly important point, for it is with the Tabernacle that the most complex sacrificial system and ritual service is associated.

In taking up this theme, we shall first note how futile some of the attempts made by the critics to explain the Tabernacle and its service, really are, and then we shall show positively that the facts associated with the Tabernacle tell against the radical theory most seriously.

First, let us note some things which the critics have to say. They are bound to face the problem, and the feats of critical gymnastics which they perform in dealing with it are somewhat entertaining. We note one or two with the utmost brevity.

First: the view that there may have been an Ark, but that there was no Tabernacle in early times is not well founded. This critical view maintains that there was only a tent called "the tent of meeting" at first, and it was not till later times, in the Priest's code, that the Tabernacle appeared. The account in Exodus is perfectly natural, if we take into account the incident of the golden calf. Because of this defection, Moses moved his tent to a distance, and this was "the tent of meeting." In due time the Tabernacle proper was prepared according to the divine model shown to Moses in the Mount. Then this Tabernacle can be traced historically during the wilderness era, and then into Canaan, and for a long period there. Consequently, the Tabernacle is not an expansion of "the tent of meeting," but a complete structure from the beginning, and it had a continuous history till it was merged into the Temple.

Secondly: the claim of radical criticism in certain quarters that the Tabernacle was a reproduction of the Temple in miniature, is utterly groundless. This supposition puts the Temple before the Tabernacle. This view is so absurd that it is scarcely worth while to take time to refute it. It is utterly opposed to the history alike of the Tabernacle and the Temple; it is inconsistent with the evolutionary principle which radical criticism applies to the development of the religion of Israel, for it puts the more elaborate Temple service before that of the Tabernacle; and finally it places the Tabernacle at the time of the Exile, a period when the Ark disappears entirely from the history, and the history itself tells us of the *rebuilding* of the Temple instead of the *construction* of the Tabernacle.

Thirdly: the contention of the radical critics that the history of the Tabernacle has been projected backward in time is without any good reasons in its support. The Mosaic origin of the Tabernacle is far harder to disprove than the Mosaic authorship of the books which tell us about it. Even though it be made out that another hand, or series of hands has written the account of the Tabernacle, it would not follow that the Tabernacle itself and the legislation connected with it were not Mosaic. Then we may not forget that the reality of the history is so definite that it can only be the stress of a preconceived theory that drives radical criticism to manipulate the history as it does.

In the second place, we now proceed to deal with some things of a positive nature connected with the Tabernacle which together make up a severe verdict against radical criticism. Our space permits us to mention only a few of these briefly.

First: it is worth while to note the fact that the description of the make-up of the Tabernacle, and the directions concerning its transportation were best suited for the wilderness career of the people. So far as the history of it is concerned, this is just what we find. It was made so that it could be easily taken down and set up; it was actually carried from place to place in the wilderness, and afterwards brought through Jordan to Canaan in the days of the judges. Then later on the Ark was at Shiloh and other places in Canaan for a time, and it is reasonable to suppose that the Tabernacle and its service was associated with the presence of the Ark in those places. To argue, as the critics do, that the Tabernacle and its service was a later product, coming into existence, long after the people were settled in Canaan and perhaps after the Temple of Solomon was built, is certainly rowing against the stream. No wonder, therefore, that these critics are inclined to regard the whole experience of the people in the wilderness as mythical.

Secondly: we remark that to give the idea of the Tabernacle a late origin is to invert the whole order of the development of the religious life of Israel and to reduce it to utter confusion. Of course, it is entirely out of harmony with the conservative view of this development, which maintains that the complete Mosaic system of ritual and legislation was the ideal before the people from the first. This view is also out of harmony with the main principles of the radical theory for it puts the Tabernacle service subsequent to the Temple, while the latter was much more elaborate than the former; and according to the natural evolutionary principle the more elaborate should come last in the order of time. Consequently, the radical theory is not only lacking in self-consistency, but is out of harmony with any reasonable view of the religious development of Israel.

Thirdly: the Tabernacle would really be of no use after the Exile, at which time radical criticism would have us believe that its idea came into existence. This criticism entirely overlooks the real historical conditions of the Exilic period. Previous to the Exile the Temple ritual, which was simply an expansion of the Tabernacle service, had been in vogue for centuries; the second Temple was built in connection with the Restoration, and the natural inference is that matters would soon settle down to the status of the period before the Exile. This would bring in the Temple ritual in its substantial form. Now in these circumstances, we simply ask, What was the use of the Tabernacle? In the settled state in Canaan there was no need for it; nor could it have a place in the religious life and observance of the people at that time. It was out of season; and so radical criticism has on its hands a complete Tabernacle which was useless and all out of date. Then, too, the fact already alluded to in this chapter in reference to the absence of any notice of the Ark after the Exile, has force here again. The main purpose of the Tabernacle was to contain the Ark of the testimony. If this Ark, as is generally admitted now, was not in existence at all at that time, what was the use of the Tabernacle? Again, it was useless, and here again; radical criticism, as so often, gives us the shell without the kernel. These points must be met by radical criticism, and we demand a proper explanation before we can allow the radical theory to be propounded without challenge.

Fourthly: the history, at certain great junctures of the nation, makes it clear that the Tabernacle existed in early times. The account of the crossing of Jordan in the days of Joshua is very clear and definite. The account of the removal of the Ark to Jerusalem by David is of as decided a historical nature as anything could possibly be. And even if no distinct mention is made that the Tabernacle then existed, the view that time had virtually brought it into decay, may be as good a reason for its seeming absence in David's day as the supposition that it did not exist at all till many years after. So in Solomon's day the history is equally clear. We simply demand of the critics a satisfactory explanation of these historical facts. We shall not be content with any fictitious account of the history, for if the history be fiction, what is to become of the doctrines? Are they fiction also? Then, above all, we claim that it would simply be impossible for any scribe, living in the time of

Josiah and Ezra, to write up the history in a purely fictitious way. The details of names, places, and dates are far too great for any such mode of production. It really requires more faith to believe that such a thing is possible in a purely natural way than to believe in the supernatural genesis of the complete Mosaic system.

Fifthly: the ritual of mature Mosaism was connected with the Tabernacle, and so if we find the Tabernacle extant at as early a date as the Conquest, then it is reasonable to conclude that the complete Levitical code was then in existence. The ritual of the day of atonement, the requirements of all the annual feasts, the details of cleansing from various forms of uncleanness, and the complex legal code were all connected with the Tabernacle and the Ark which it contained. This gave a single sanctuary as the law of the religious system from the beginning. And when we find, as we do, that the Tabernacle is alluded to in the literature of all the so-called codes, there is surely good reason for concluding that all these codes existed from the first, and are to be regarded as a complex unit, and not a series of successive codes increasing in complexity and coming into existence gradually. The force of this argument will be made much greater after we discuss in the next chapter the great feasts of the Mosaic system. We now content ourselves with pointing out the fact that the Tabernacle existed from early times in Israel, and with indicating the view that the mature ritual and sacrificial system of the people were associated with the Tabernacle, and hence must have really existed from the first.

In closing this chapter, we remark that it is evident that the argument from the Tabernacle and its ritual, tells with terrible effect against radical criticism. The effort of that criticism to account for the Tabernacle and all that pertained to it in harmony with its theory, must be pronounced a signal failure, while conservative criticism has little difficulty in keeping possession of the field with a reasonable explanation of all the facts in the case. The apostle in Hebrews tells us that "there was a Tabernacle made," and there it stands as a perpetual challenge to radical criticism

CHAPTER XI.

THE GREAT FEASTS.

FROM the consideration of the Tabernacle and the priesthood, we pass in this chapter to a brief study of the great *feasts* of the Mosaic system, and our endeavor will be to examine, in as careful a manner as our limits allow, the views and theories of advanced critics upon this particular subject.

It need scarcely be remarked in entering upon this topic, that we have before us a large and difficult subject. For those who wish to pursue study at length on this topic we know of no better guide than the able and learned discussion of it in "The Hebrew Feasts," by Dr. W. Henry Green, of Princton, N. J., than whom there is no more competent scholar at the present day in the Old Testament field.

The advanced critics claim that from the way the Jewish feasts are spoken of in the different so-called codes, there are many things to support their theories and conclusions. They point out the fact that certain of these feasts are barely mentioned in the Deuteronomic code, and that the ritual of the great day of atonement is described only in what is called by the critics the Priests' code. From this

THE GREAT FEASTS. 243

it is argued that the elaborate system of feasts in the religion of Israel did not exist from the first, but came gradually into existence among the people. These feasts as they finally appeared were not Mosiac in their origin and contents, but were the product of later religious development among the people, which became complete only about the time of the Exile.

In support of this radical view the critics are not content to reason merely from the allusions to these feasts in the Scriptures. The critics take us on interesting excursions among pagan customs, and describe to us in a very eloquent way how these Jewish feasts are to be understood as natural developments from various nature festivals. These feasts thus rest largely upon a natural agricultural and pastoral basis, and may all be traced back, so the critics assure us, to the customs of the tribes who dwelt in Canaan before them. By a simple and natural process these festivals were transferred from Baal and other deities to Jehovah, and as worship was gradually centralized in one place, these feasts gradually assumed their distinct Jewish forms. The germs of this result are found in Deuteronomy, but the complete development only appears in the days of Ezra.

In making criticism of the radical position in regard to the great feasts, we shall follow two lines, dwelling chiefly on the second of these. We shall first examine the *natural* explanation of the feasts given by the critics ; and secondly, we shall endeavor to show that the critical contention is not supported from the contents of the Scriptures, even if we allow that there are three codes in the Old Testament literature.

In regard to the first line of inquiry we need not say very much. It will be observed that the critical procedure here consists simply in applying the principle of natural evolution to the development of the feasts of Israel's religion. According to this principle, simple nature festivals, connected with vintage and harvest, gradually grew into the elaborate ritual of the great Jewish feasts. Now we allege here that the critics adduce no sufficient proof of their position at this point. They simply assume that the religion of Israel was a simple, natural product like other religious systems, and then make the transition from the customs of the Canaanites to the festivals of the Israelites without any adequate historical basis on which to stand, and without adducing any sufficient facts to prove their position. If what we have said in a former chapter on the philosophy of religion be recalled, it will serve as a complete refutation of the critical claims at this important point. Even if we admit that the Jewish feasts were associated with certain processes in nature, it by no means follows that there was no supernatural element in them, or that they were not unique in their nature.

THE GREAT FEASTS. 245

But we proceed to the second point, and seek to show that the true view of the great feasts tells against the critical theory rather than in favor of it. Our readers will remember that the annual feasts of the Israelites were seven in number, and they were divided into at least two cycles. They were the following: The Passover, followed closely by the Feast of Unleavened Bread, the Feast of Weeks, the Feast of Trumpets or New Moon, the Day of Atonement, the Feast of Tabernacles, and a Solemn Assembly at the close of the Feast of Tabernacles.

We cannot speak of all of these in this chapter, so we select three of the most familiar and important of the seven, and discuss their bearing on the views of advanced criticism. These three are the Passover, the Feast of Weeks, and the Feast of Tabernacles. This gives us really the Passover, Pentecost, and Tabernacles, with which we are made familiar both in Old Testament and New.

Just a word may be said in explanation of these three great annual feasts. The Passover originated in connection with the departure from Egypt, and was observed in memory of the deliverance of the people from the house of bondage.

The Feast of Weeks, or, as it is usually termed in the New Testament, the Day of Pentecost, was fifty days after the Passover. This feast was at the end of harvest, and consisted mainly in an offering of the first fruits of the harvest, in various forms, unto the Lord.

The Feast of Tabernacles came five days after the Day of Atonement. There seem to have been two elements in this feast. First, the dwelling of the people in booths in memory of the wilderness journey, and, secondly, the ingathering of the fruits. It was thus the harvest-home of Israel.

Now it is contended by radical critics that these various feasts were late products of the religion of Israel, and that they grew gradually out of old customs connected with the season of the year, and the products of agriculture. They were nature festivals transformed into definite religious rites. Two of these — Pentecost and Tabernacles — were associated with harvest, the one at the beginning and the other at the close of the ingathering. If any Jewish feasts are capable of being explained, as the radical critics contend; and if any can be shown not to have come into existence until late in the history of the Jews, these are the ones. Hence, if we make inquiry concerning these, and can show that they existed from early days, a good case is made out against the radical critics. Unless history be turned upside down, this can be easily shown from the sacred records themselves.

In the first place, the argument from silence proves nothing, or it proves too much, regarding the feasts just as we have already seen in regard to other things in this discussion. If in the Covenant

THE GREAT FEASTS. 247

and Deuteronomic codes we do not find much concerning some of these feasts, it does not follow that they did not exist. This point has been so elaborated in a former chapter, concerning another matter, that it need only be mentioned here. It may be well to add, however, that if silence, or absence of mention in the history of Israel of any rite or ceremony, proves anything, it would be hard to prove that the Day of Atonement was observed till some time after the days of Ezra. From allusions in other parts of Scripture, it is clear that this solemn feast was observed. Hence, the assumption of the critics concerning the silence of the historical narrative proves too much, and that is the same as proving nothing in this case.

In the second place, each of the feasts, according to the biblical view, has a definite time set for its origin and observance. The Passover was the fourteenth day of Nisan, Pentecost was fifty days after, and Tabernacles at the close of harvest. In this connection it is well to remember the commemorative nature of these feasts, which gives still clearer definiteness in time to the origin of these feasts according to the biblical view. According to the advanced critical theory, all is vague and indefinite. The critics cannot tell us definitely, nor do they agree in their views, as to the time and circumstances of the origin of these feasts, if they are the product of natural development. At this point, therefore, the critical theory so lacks definiteness that when compared with the biblical account, it fails to commend itself as based on historical fact, or as a proper explanation of the facts.

In the third place, the purpose of the feasts is more fully and naturally explained according to the bibical view, and this again tells strongly against the radical theory. The main purpose of the Passover was to commemorate the wonderful way in which the Lord, by a high hand, brought the people out of Egypt. We would naturally expect that as such it would date from the time of that deliverance. The radical theory which makes it later, has really no reason in it, for what sense would there be in beginning to observe this great event in the history of the people centuries after its occurrence? So in regard to the commemorative element in the Feast of Tabernacles, which related to the wilderness wandering. There is no reason in the view of radical criticism which gives this also a late origin centuries after the era of that wandering. We would expect just what the biblical view presents, and that is its observance from the first. So in regard to the *harvest* element in Pentecost and Tabernacles. It is not reasonable to suppose that the people had gone on gathering harvests for centuries in Canaan before these elements came into existence. We would expect them from the first. And, moreover, we find harvest elements in these feasts in their mature form. If these feasts grew out of old nature festivals, we would expect these elements to have been largely eliminated. Then, too, there are some feasts, especially the Passover and Day of Atonement, in which there are no signs of nature factors, and to which there is nothing similar in any of the customs of the Canaanites of which we know anything.

In the fourth place, it would be easy to show, did space permit, that these feasts existed by divine appointment from the Mosaic era. By the history, by the prophets, by the Psalms, by the New Testament allusions, this could be made perfectly plain. We would, instead of following out these several lines at length, refer our readers to Dr. Green's "Hebrew Feasts" for further discussion of this subject, and for refutation of the radical critical theory. Our conviction is that a careful study of these feasts will show that the radical theory introduces disorder into the sequence of the feasts, does injustice to the Mosaic system, and utterly ignores the history which they imply. In a word, the feasts are a puzzle on the radical critical theory.

CHAPTER XII.

THE PROPHETS.

In this chapter we have to consider a topic of great importance in itself, and of deep significance in relation to the modern critical views under debate in this little work. What is the precise place and function of the prophetic order in the religion of Israel, and what is the relation of the prophets to the law and ritual of the Mosaic system, are questions earnestly discussed by biblical scholars at the present day. We would naturally expect that such a subject should be taken hold of by the radical critics in support of their peculiar theory.

We have already seen what position radical criticism assumes in regard to the prophets and their work. In general, the critics contend that the prophets came before the fully developed Mosaic law and ritual arose, and by their influence much was done to produce ethical monotheism, and to pave the way for worship at one central sanctuary. Moreover, the critics of the radical school usually minimize the predictive element in the prophetic writings, and some of them are bold enough to deny this element altogether. The critics, also,

THE PROPHETS.   251

in order to make their views plausible, seek to bring much of the prophetic literature down to later times, on the ground that in the early stages of the religious life of Israel such maturity of religious ideas as is found in the prophetic writings, could not have existed among the people.

The main point now to be considered is the relation of the Prophets to the Law. Which was first in order? Did the law exist first, and was the great work of the prophets to keep the people in obedience to this law, or call them back when they went astray from it? Or, did the prophets precede the law, in its mature form at least? And was the great work of the prophets to originate among the people ethic monotheism, and to develop worship at one sanctuary, and so prepare the way for mature Mosaism in the days of Josiah and Ezra? The latter is the view of radical critics. The former is the view we propose to defend against them. We can only suggest a few lines of remark without following out any one of them at length.

In the first place, the assumed silence of the prophets, even if true, would not establish the conclusions of advanced criticism. This is the argument, *a silentio* again; and, as we have noted its invalidity at other points, we need only mention it here. Even if in the days of the prophets the law was not observed, it does not follow that it was not then binding, and, of course, existent, for declension and apostasy may often have been the explanation of its non-observance ; and, even when uniformly observed by the people, there was no need that the prophets should formally and repeatedly be expounding the contents of a law regularly observed. In either of these cases we would scarcely expect to find anything else or anything more than we do in the prophetic utterances. The great stress, therefore, which the critics lay on the silence of the prophets, even if true to the extent they represent, would not justify them in placing the prophets prior to the law.

In the second place, if the principle of natural development be relied on, as it is so largely by the radical critics, then these critics must face the difficulty of showing how the law in its mature form developed from the prophets and what they taught. Let it be remembered that the critics emphasize that some of the early prophets seem to lift up their voices aloud against elaborate ritual and sacrifice, for the purpose of showing that the mature Mosaic ritual did not exist in their day. Now we simply ask the critics how, on their naturalistic principles and in accordance with the view they give of the attitude of the prophets toward ritual, any development in the direction of an elaborate ritual system could possibly have taken place. If the prophets are opposed to elaborate ritual, how could they have aided in producing mature Mosaism, which has a complete ritual and sacrificial system

THE PROPHETS. 253

contained in it. The view that the law was first with its complete ritual is much more natural. It is easier to explain the prophets from the law, than the law from the prophets. This position is of vital importance in the discussion.

In the third place, the burden of the prophetic message oftentimes was to call the people back to an old and neglected law. To quote the passages which bear upon this point would be to take up the space of a whole chapter. Amos, Joel, Hosea and Isaiah abound in these passages. Jeremiah also has many things which show how the people had declined from the early ideal, and how he earnestly called the people back. In Hosea alone there is more than enough to refute the contentions of the radical critics at this point. The figure of the unfaithful spouse, and the earnest calls to this spouse to return to her first proper affection, illustrate the function of the prophets in the age prior to Josiah about one hundred and twenty years, and before the days of Ezra fully three hundred years. From such facts as these, scattered all through the pre-exilian prophets, the conclusion is evident that the mature Mosaic system of law and ritual existed prior to the prophets, and before the date given by radical critics for the origin of the Deuteronomic and Priestly codes. In other words, it is impossible to interpret the prophets unless we assume the existence of the complete legal and ritual system. The prophets did not profess to be propounding some new way, but were calling the wayward people back to the old forgotten paths of their fathers. The meaning of all this is that the fully developed ritual was prior to the prophets, instead of the reverse as the critics contend.

In the fourth place, we find in the pre-exilian prophets frequent allusions to the deliverance from Egypt, and to the history of the people of Israel as recorded in the historical books, and that as they stand in the Old Testament without reconstruction by the critics. The radical theory concerning the place and functions of the prophets cannot be harmonized with the history found in Kings and Chronicles. Hence, the critics maintain that the history must be reconstructed in accordance with the terms of their theory regarding the prophets. But this is surely unnecessary if we can harmonize another and simpler view of the prophetic writings with the contents of the historical books. Hence, the conclusion may be securely held against radical criticism that the prophets presuppose the history just as it stands. The historical allusions so abundant in the prophetic writings would have no meaning according to the radical views of certain critics. And this is true not only of the historical references to the people of Israel, but, also, of the many allusions found in the prophets to the history of the surrounding nations. If the radical theory of the prophets be held, violence is done to the history. But when mere theory comes into conflict with historic facts, we prefer to hold by the facts and shape our theory accordingly. We commend this line of refutation of radical criticism to the attention of those who would follow it out at length.

In the fifth place, we find the prophets of the centuries prior to the Exile insisting on worship at a single central sanctuary. Even the prophets of the northern kingdom, like Hosea and Amos, do this. Now the radical critics contend that in this we are to find the germ of that worship at a single sanctuary which is set forth in the Priests' code. In our judgment, the far more natural view is that the fact of worship at one central shrine was the law from the first, that the people often forgot this, and worshiped where they ought not to have rendered such service, and that the great task of the prophets was to call the people back to the ideal of days gone by, which implied that the worship of the people was to be rendered to one God at one central sanctuary, and that was where the Tabernacle was planted, and where the Temple in later days was built and furnished.

In the sixth place, we contend that the prophets did not originate ethic monotheism, as the critics assume. They simply taught on this subject what was more or less definitely the historical faith of the people from the Mosaic era. The Covenant code very distinctly announced monotheism with which ethical ideas were necessarily connected. This ideal expressed in the ten commandments was the ideal of the people from the first. They may often have fallen far short of the ideal, but it was ever before them. When they fell into idolatry, the people were punished, pardoned, and restored. Now, the great work of the prophets in this connection was not to generate ethic monotheism, but to call back the people in the name of God and by his authority to the ideal of ethic monotheism to which they were committed from the beginning of their remarkable career. Even a cursory reading of the prophets will confirm this view.

In the seventh place, the contention of the critics in certain quarters that the prophets could not have lived and written as early as the conservative view holds that they did, because of the advanced ideas they exhibited, is ill-founded. Ultra-radical critics make much of this point in seeking to discredit the contents of the prophetic writings. But a moment's reflection will show the absurdity of this view. Take the ideas expressed in those Psalms which are Davidic in origin and produced three hundred years before the early writing prophets, and note the deep and intense religious ideas and expressions found in these Psalms. Take the book of Job, which in spite of the critics, may still be held to be of great antiquity, and note the lofty religious conceptions presented therein. Or take the songs of Moses, as found in the 90th Psalm, and in the closing chapters of Deuteronomy, and who shall say that even the greatest of the prophets have risen to loftier heights of religious thought and expression than we find in these songs. Of course, when the critics proceed to tell us that these songs were not uttered by Moses, but put in his mouth by men of centuries later, we simply demand ample proof for such a preposterous assumption. To argue to what actually was, from what the critics think ought to have been, is simply absurd.

In the last place, the pre-exilian prophets abound in allusions to the details of the mature Mosaic law to such an extent and in such a manner, that we are simply shut up to the conclusion, that, when they wrote, the complete Priests' code was already in existence among the people. In Hosea, in Amos, in Joel, in Isaiah, and in Jeremiah, all of whom lived and wrote before the days of Ezra, and most of whom date prior to Josiah, we find allusion to the priesthood, to the sacrifices in detail, to the one sanctuary, to the distinction between the clean and unclean, in a way that is inexplicable, if the Priests' code was not familiar to these prophets. This is a mine in which the conservative critic may do good work, and get great gain in favor of his views. A careful study of the prophets in the light of radical criticism will give fine results in itself, and provide us with abundant material with which to refute radical criticism at this point in the discussion.

CHAPTER XIII.

THE PSALMS.

IN the discussions of this chapter we pass from the Law and the Prophets to the *Psalms*. In doing so we come to a wide theme which bears very directly upon the matters in debate between radical and conservative criticism. During recent years, the exposition of the Psalter in the light of advanced critical theories of the religion of Israel has engaged earnest attention. Advanced criticism has striven to deprive David and his age of the honor of producing many of the Psalms, and some recent critics seek to show that nearly the whole of the Psalter originated after the Exile. By such critics it is described as the Praise-book of the second temple, rather than, in its leading parts, the Psalter of the first temple. In this chapter we seek to deal with the Psalms in relation to the advanced critical theories now under review.

In the first place, we remark that the critics have not yet succeeded in depriving David and others of his age of the honor of the authorship of the great body of the Psalms. The burden of proof, moreover, lies with the critics at this point, and unless they can make out a case against the greater part of the Psalms usually ascribed to David's age, enough will remain to justify conclusions against radical criticism at this point. We freely admit that the titles or superscriptions of the Psalms may not be inspired; and yet we maintain that the radical critics must show how it came to pass that in the Hebrew texts these titles often stand as the first verse of the Psalms. But even though they may not be inspired, these titles have the very highest value as historical evidence, which can only be justly set aside by similar evidence of a higher value. Till such evidence is adduced, we may give value to the titles in favor of authorship. This enables us to place the bulk of the Psalter in David's age, and in connection with the temple of Solomon. We are prepared also to maintain that even if the critics can show that some of the titles are incorrect, there will still remain enough of the contents of the Psalter admitted to be Davidic in its origin, to enable us to overthrow the main positions of the radical theories in regard to the development of the religion of Israel. It is proper to add that the radical critics have not yet shown that in those Psalms which by their titles are ascribed to the Davidic age, there are contained any matters or references inconsistent with their origin in that age. This negative position has no little value against the critical theories.

In the second place, we remark that in the Psalms generally, there are such frequent and definite allusions to the history of Israel, as suffice to refute the radical theories which undertake to reconstruct that history, in accordance with a preconceived theory. We cannot make full quotations here, but a few examples will suffice to illustrate what we mean. In Ps. 77 : 16-20, we have distinct allusion to the deliverance from Egypt, the passage of the Red Sea, and the Wilderness wandering. In Ps. 78 : 13-20, the reference to the same great facts is even clearer. Indeed this whole Psalm which is ascribed to Asaph, of David's age, is as clear a testimony to the historicity of the early career of Israel as can be desired. To resolve it into poetic myth is simply absurd. In Ps. 81 : 10, the Exodus from Egypt is again referred to. The whole of Psalms 105 and 106, deserves to be read and studied in this connection. The entire outline of the history of Israel is virtually recited in these Psalms. So also Psalms 114, 132, 135, and 136, bear similar testimony. We ask our readers to ponder these Psalms carefully, simply in relation to the history which they assume or imply, and then to raise the question whether these historical allusions can possibly be fictitious, or written up long after as the mere filling in of the ritual scheme, as radical criticism contends.

Now, our purpose in adducing the historic implications of the Psalms, is to show that the Psalms assume the history as a fact, and that we have testimony of the very highest value in them to the history of Israel, not as conceived by radical criticism, but as set forth in the Scriptures, and as maintained by conservative criticism. And, further, it deserves to be borne in mind in the same connection, that if the conservative view of the history is confirmed, then the two go together.

It is no wonder that radical criticism makes war on the history, for unless it can justify historical reconstruction, it cannot by any ingenuity make out its theory of the origin and growth of religious ideas and practices. But at this point we bring the critics face to face with the historical allusions in the Psalms, and demand an explanation of these at their hands. Even if we admit that the whole Psalter was *post-exilic*, the case would not be materially altered, for we have historical confirmation by the writers of that age, and by inspired men too, of the main outlines of the history of Israel in a way incapable of reconciliation with radical theories. The Psalms of Davidic origin very definitely register the views of the preceding history prevalent at that day. Is it possible that the critics of the present day can know more about the history than David and Asaph did?

In the third place, we take the position that the advanced degree of religious thought and sentiment, set forth in the Psalms, is far beyond what was possible at the Davidic era according to the radical critics. This indeed the radical critics assert, but our interpretation of the facts here is entirely different from theirs. They tell us that the Psalms could not have been the product of David or his age, because the development of religious ideas had not reached such a stage at his day. Hence we are told that the Psalms must belong to the age when the development of ritual and legislation was complete. This puts them at and after the Exile.

The position we take here in opposition to the critics is that we admit with them the lofty spiritual ideas and the deep religious sentiments which the Psalms exhibit, but we maintain on historical ground, not on a theoretical basis, that this religious stage was attained at David's day. This is the natural view of the biblical narratives, and it harmonizes fully with the conservative position, which holds that the mature Mosaic system was set forth for the people soon after the Exodus, and prior to the conquest. With this lofty ideal before them, the people were led on in religious knowledge and life, and in this way they could have had no difficulty in making the attainments in the age of David, which we find expressed in the Psalms. Moreover, the radical theory, as we have already seen, based on the evolutionary idea, takes too low a view of the actual religious condition of the Israelites at the time they left Egypt. It is compelled to do this by the stern necessities of its own theory. The true history as vindicated by the Psalms, affords a basis to explain the high religious contents of the Psalms, without the assumption that the Psalms are to be regarded as of a late origin. The biblical view is quite natural, while the critical theory is very unnatural.

In the fourth place, we further contend in close connection with the preceding point, that even if the Psalms were *post-exilic* to a very large extent, they do not really reflect the character of that age. If they were the product of that age, as the critics say, we would expect to find in them the special features of the age of the Exile. But there is no reason to believe, even on the critical theory, that there was any deeper religious sentiment prevalent among the people in Ezra's day than in the age of David. The critics themselves seldom press their argument at this point. According to that theory there was elaboration of ritual ; but it does not follow that there was expansion of spiritual life. Perhaps the opposite is true, and that after the Exile, the rabbinical spirit, tending to formality rather than to spirituality, arose.

There is no reason to believe that the prophetic writings of the age of the Exile show a deeper religious experience than we find in the prophets near David's age. And it is very clear, even to the plain uncritical reader, that those Psalms which are claimed to be *post-exilic* do not show any deeper religious sentiment than those which even radical critics admit to be Davidic in origin. The critics are bound to show that there was this advance.

Then add to this the fact that the Psalms in general do not show any sympathy with, nor reflect in any degree the spirit of, the Persian age, or of the rabbinical spirit which soon after arose, and we have a strong case against advanced criticism regarding the Psalms and their place in the religious development of Israel.

In the fifth place, the Psalms uniformly teach ethical monotheism, and worship at one central sanctuary. This is so evident that we need scarcely cite proofs. One God, the only living and true God, is to be worshiped, idolatry is constantly condemned, and one sanctuary emphasized as the proper place of worship. The critics cannot deny this, but they hope to escape its force by the *postexilic* theory of the origin of the most of the Psalms. If, therefore, we make out the Davidic origin of the greater part of the Psalter, and vindicate the real nature of the historical allusions contained therein, as we think we have done, then ethical monotheism, the condemnation of idol worship, and the obligation to worship at a single sanctuary, all existed as a matter of fact in David's age. This tells forcibly against radical criticism at an important point. The following passages may be consulted in support of our position: Ps. 9 : 11 ; 11 : 4 ; 20 : 2 ; 24 : 7 ; 27 : 4 ; 48 : 2, 3 ; 63 : 2 ; 76 : 2 ; 77 : 13. These passages all refer to a single sanctuary. And observe that most of them are from Psalms which have strong claims to belong to David's age. Nor can the critics show that greater emphasis is laid upon worship at a single sanctuary in the Psalms of the age of the Exile. To quote passages against idol worship and in favor of monotheism is unnecessary. We merely refer to Psalm 115 in passing.

In the last place, the Psalms viewed generally presuppose at almost every turn the Mosaic ritual and legislation; and we maintain that they cannot be squared with any theory that would find their origin in any other supposition than that the Psalms reflect the Mosaic spirit in its mature stage. This is a very wide field. It indeed affords material for a whole treatise, so that we can only signalize it in closing this chapter. In the Psalms of David's age, as fully as anywhere else, we find allusions to the Mosaic sacrifices, to the Feasts, to the Tabernacle, and to the Priests in a way which is simply inexplicable on the radical theory. We wish that we had space to work this out fully. We only mark out the lines briefly, and leave the reader to fill out further particulars.

As to ritual and sacrifice, see Ps. 26:6; 40:6; 50:5; 51:7; 66:13-15. In these and similar passages we have references to those offerings which are found in all the so-called codes of the radical critics, at or near the age of David.

As to the Tabernacle and the Temple, see Ps. 15:1; 27:5; 28:2; 42:4; 43:3, 4; 46:4; 63:2; 65:1-3. These are but a few passages which show the existence of the Tabernacle and Temple, and with them mature Mosaism, at least at the time of David, centuries prior to the date assigned to it by the radical critics.

As to the priesthood, we quote the following: Ps. 87 : 64 ; 99 : 6 ; 115 : 10 ; 122 ; 132 : 9–16 ; 133 ; 135 : 20. These Psalms allude to the priesthood in such a way as to bring out the view that it was then a complete graded system. Hence, unless the radical critics can make good the claim that these passages are all *post-exilic* in their origin, there is much force in them against the radical critical theories.

Finally, there are frequent allusions to a *covenant* and a *law*, terms which presuppose the Mosaic scheme. Then there are words and phrases in the Psalms which seem to be drawn from the complete Mosaic system. Such are the terms: *banners, glory, goodly heritage, shadow of the wings, congregation*. These and similar phrases indicate how completely the spirit of the mature Mosaic system is reflected in the Psalms. Without this system the Psalms could scarcely be what they are, and we may justly ask radical criticism for an explanation.

CHAPTER XIV.

THE GOSPEL NARRATIVES.

HAVING virtually completed the discussions arising from the contents of the Old Testament in their bearing upon the conclusions of radical criticism, we pass in this chapter to consider some things of vital importance to the questions raised, which emerge from a perusal of the New Testament. This chapter will deal specially with the *Gospel narratives*. Here the most prominent feature is the view which our Lord himself took of the Old Testament, and the religious system which it unfolds.

If he took certain views, the question is: How are these to be understood and explained? And so, in like manner, in regard to those passages in the Gospels which come from their inspired authors: How are we to regard their interpretation of the Old Testament History and religious system? These questions indicate at once how important the Gospel narratives, and especially the teaching of our Lord, become in the adequate discussion of the questions in debate between radical and conservative criticism. Some care, then, must be exercised in their treatment, for the whole question of the way in which Jesus understood and expounded the Old Testament history and ritual is here involved. It is evident also that the *accommodation* and *kenosis* theories in regard to the earthly career of our Lord are also in sight in the reasonings of the radical critics, as they attempt to turn the edge of the teaching of the great Teacher away from their reconstructive theories of the Mosaic system. We deal with several points in order in this chapter, and shall conclude it with some brief notice of the consequences which follow from the views of the radical critics in relation to the person of Christ.

In the first place, there are in the Gospels such plain and definite references to the history of the Old Testament, that the reconstructive theories of the advanced critics cannot be reconciled therewith. In other words, the views of the history of the Old Testament period given in the Gospels agree with the opinions of conservative critics, which simply means that these opinions best represent the views set forth in the Gospel history.

In Matt. 11 : 21–24 there is allusion to Tyre and Sidon, and especially to Sodom, which agrees entirely with the history of the Old Testament. In Matt. 12 : 3, there is reference to David and the shewbread, which shows that our Lord endorsed the view, that in the days of David the Tabernacle service and the Priestly code were in vogue. In Matt. 12 : 40, 41, our Lord confirms the historicity of the case of Jonah and the great fish, and uses it as an emblem of his own resurrection. In Matt. 24 : 37, the history of Noah is confirmed, together with the reality of the deluge. There is no hint at myth or reconstruction here whatever.

In Mark 3 : 8 ; 6 : 11 ; 12 : 26–36 ; in Luke 4 : 26, 27 ; 11 : 30–51 ; 17 : 26–32 ; 20 : 37 ; and in John 3 : 14 ; 6 : 31, there are similar references to important facts in the history of Israel. They are nearly all made by our Lord himself, and are unique in that respect. From them we conclude that it is clear that our Lord did not hold views in harmony with modern radical critics. Our Lord not only confirms the natural historical view of the Old Testament, but he also binds these facts to some of the great doctrines he taught, in such a way as to cause the fact and the doctrine to stand or fall together. The lifting up of the serpent in the wilderness and the death of Christ ; the case of Jonah and His resurrection ; the experience of Noah and the end of the world, illustrate this feature of the way in which our Lord used Old Testament history. How puerile the radical theories, which reduce these facts to something little better than myths, seem beside the methods of our Lord here !

In the second place, the Gospels uniformly ascribe the Old Testament law and ritual to a Mosaic origin. Our Lord does this constantly, so much so that if the radical critics are right, he either blundered, or intentionally took the prevalent though erroneous view. A few passages will illustrate the case in hand.

In Matt. 19:7, we read concerning divorce, "Why did *Moses* then command, etc.," where the reference is to the Deuteronomic code. In Mark 10:3, we have the same reference. In Mark 12:19, concerning marrying a brother's wife, we read, "Master, *Moses wrote;*" and although these are the words of Sadducees, Jesus did not contradict them, or state that they were in error on that point. In Luke 20:28, we have the same thing. In Luke 24:27, we have reference to "Moses and all the prophets," made by Jesus after his resurrection, in a way which suggests the Mosaic origin of the law. So in John 5:45; 7:19; 8:5, we have allusions to the law of Moses, in terms which leave no room to doubt that, rightly or wrongly, our Lord ascribed the Old Testament ritual and legislation to a Mosaic origin, at least in the sense that it arose in that age. Here again the critics have a serious task to deal with, and we shall see, later on, how they attempt to handle it. Our Lord clearly assumes a Mosaic genesis for the whole system which was known as the "Law of Moses" in his day. This testimony is of prime importance and value.

In the third place, there are in the Gospels such references to the priests, and to the Levitical system, as justify us in maintaining that the critical theory of a graded priesthood, of different documents, and of three distinct codes, is not supported by the view of the Old Testament religion presented in the Gospels. In other words, the Gospel view is that there was a peculiar unity and a completeness from the first in the Mosaic system. This point can only be briefly illustrated.

In Matt. 5 : 23, 24, we have a matter referred to which belongs to what the critics call the Deuteronomic code, in regard to bringing the gift to the altar, and being reconciled to our brother. In Matt. 8 : 4, where the case of the leper is described, allusion is made to the contents of the Priestly code, as the critics would say. So also in Matt. 21 : 15 ; 26 : 3, 14, 17 ; 27: 20 ; in Mark 2 : 25 ; 10 : 18–27; in Luke 2 : 22 ; 4 : 3, 4 ; 5 : 14 ; 20 : 19, we have allusions to various elements in the Mosaic system, such as the priests, the feasts, the cleansings, and the sacrifices, which are significant in this connection. We are sure that any candid and reverent study of these passages will show that the radical critical theory requires us to give a strangely forced meaning to every one of them. The point we emphasize is that the Gospel narratives, and especially the words of our Lord, know nothing whatever of the necessity of a reconstructed Old Testament, or of a diversity of ritual and legal codes which only came gradually into existence. And further, in one or two cases our Lord hints that this was the ideal state which was before the people from the first for their observance. In regard to divorce, he says,

"From the beginning it was not so," which surely indicates that the development theory of the radical critics is not the true key to unlock the problem of the religion of Israel. The first stage was the ideal, and the second was a lower stage, not a higher. For ourselves, we are inclined to prefer the authoritative interpretation of the religious system of Israel made by the great Teacher, to the vague and ill-digested theorizings of the radical critics. And we shall do well to be careful that no view which shall dishonor our Lord is forced upon us by the relentless demands of a mere theory.

In the fourth place, a passing reference may be made to the bearing of the contents of the gospel on the radical theory in reference to the book of Isaiah. As our readers are aware, the critics divide this book into two parts, and give the latter section — 40 to 66 — a later origin and a different author. The important passages here are the following: Matt. 4:14-16; 8:17; 12:17; 15:7; Mark 7:6; Luke 3:4; John 12:38. From these passages, it is evident that the writers of the Gospels, and our Lord whose words are herein quoted, knew nothing of a *deutero*-Isaiah. The whole book was evidently viewed by them as a unit, and was called by the title "Isaiah." The quotations and references made by our Lord himself from the latter part of the book are ascribed to Isaiah in a way which leaves little doubt in the mind of the reader as to what was his view of these sections of

Isaiah. Now the burden of proof clearly rests with the radical critics, not only to show that this part of the prophecy could not have originated in Isaiah's day, but also to present another author who will meet the demands of the case as the author of the second Isaiah. Mere destructive criticism offering no reconstruction, mere denial of a given authorship without also providing another, can never be satisfactory nor sufficient. As against our Lord, the radical critics must do much more than they have done before they shall have made out their case against the unity of Isaiah.

In the fifth place, it is worth while noting the fact that while in the Gospel age the Priests' code, as the critics would say, ruled completely the religious life of the Jews, yet in the Gospel narratives, there is no more allusion to its existence in these narratives than there is in the earlier books of the Old Testament to its existence at that time. Now, if we allow the critical argument of "non-existence because of silence" to have weight in regard to that early age, it has equal weight in reference to the Gospel age, and would in like manner prove the non-existence of the mature Mosaic system in that age. We have seen, however, that the historical and other allusions in both ages prove its continuous existence, and thus again we see that the argument *a silentio* proves too much or too little, and so has no force whatever. This consideration is pertinent, even if we take into account the fact that the Gospels were not written in the interests of the Jewish religion. The mere historical allusions in the Gospels to the Mosaic code is all we need, to make good our position at this point, and to show the illogical methods of radical criticism, in dealing with the Gospel history.

In the last place, the attempt of radical criticism to get rid of the argument against its conclusions from the Gospels, may be described as a frantic failure. The real debate here relates to the testimony of our Lord. How can this be squared with radical criticism? Two main efforts have been made by the critics. The one is a phase of the *accommodation theory*, and the other arises from an application of the *modern kenosis theory* in regard to the person of Christ. We cannot discuss these theories at length, but can only point out the straits to which radical criticism is driven at these two points.

In regard to the first, the critics seek to show that our Lord in his allusions to the Old Testament, either fell unconsciously into the prevalent errors of the age in reference to the nature of the religious system of Israel, or purposely accommodated his teaching to views of that system which he knew to be erroneous. In either case radical criticism must rise and explain. If our Lord was ignorant, how is this to be harmonized with his knowledge; if he knowingly endorsed an error, how then is his integrity to be preserved? We simply leave these ques-

THE GOSPEL NARRATIVES. 275

tions with the radical critics, and await their resolution of the dilemma. In addition it further devolves upon radical criticism to show that the popular view of the Old Testament which existed in our Lord's day was as far astray as this criticism assumes. Even if led astray in some things by the traditions of the fathers, it does not follow that its errors confirm advanced criticism.

Touching the modern *kenosis* theory we can only remark that on doctrinal grounds we believe it to be as dangerous as the older *kenosis* doctrine of our Lord's person. Even if, therefore, advanced criticism demands for its explanation the *kenosis* idea, it may be that the support of a mere critical hypothesis has been purchased at the cost of clear scriptural views of the deity of our Lord. If the Son of God *so became* the Son of man that he was no longer truly the Son of God, and consequently but a man in his interpretation of the Old Testament and its religion, we charge radical criticism with procuring its vindication by betraying the true doctrine of our Lord's divinity in order to obviate the force of our Lord's testimony against its theory of the religion of Israel. At this stage we simply await the further explanation which advanced criticism is bound to give of the Gospel witness, and the unique testimony of our Lord.

CHAPTER XV.

OTHER NEW TESTAMENT BOOKS.

HAVING in the last chapter dealt with the Gospel narratives in their relation to radical criticism, we now proceed to gather up a few things from the other books of the New Testament, in order to see what their teaching is concerning the debate between radical and conservative criticism. The exposition can only touch in a hurried way a few salient points. The main sections of the New Testament which are of importance here are the Acts, Romans, Galatians, and Hebrews. In these books we find many allusions to the history of Israel, to their system of ritual and legislation, and to the manner of its origin and growth, which in our judgment cannot be easily reconciled with the conclusions of radical criticism. Indeed, we are quite willing to take the Epistle to the Hebrews alone as affording a complete refutation of the radical theories from the standpoint of the New Testament. This epistle, and the address of Stephen have not, so far as we are aware, been explained in a satisfactory way in harmony with the main positions of radical criticism. But let us see a few points which may go far to justify the claims of conservative criticism.

In the first place, from the Acts we can gather some important facts. In chapter 3 : 22-26, we have the words of Peter in regard to the teaching of the prophets concerning Jesus. Here Peter evidently held to views of the history of Israel and Abrahamic covenant different from those advanced by radical critics. In chapter 1 : 16 ; 2 : 25-34 ; 4 : 25-28, we have references to the Psalms, made by Peter chiefly, which assign important Psalms to David, and by implication the bulk of them to his age. In chapter 6 : 11-14; 15 : 21 ; 21 : 21 ; 28 : 23, we have the clear teaching of Peter and Paul as to the Mosaic origin of the whole law and ritual connected with his name. These passages deserve careful study since they show what these two inspired apostles taught in regard to the unity and Mosaic origin of the whole religious system of the Old Testament. This teaching, if it means anything in relation to the debate between radical and conservative criticism, is a complete refutation of the former. It entirely ignores it, and knows nothing about it. Again, in chapter 13 : 39 ; 15 : 5; 18 : 15 ; 24 : 14 ; 28 : 17, we have references to important details the Mosaic ritual made in such a manner as to connect it all with the name and age of Moses, and to present it as a well-defined unit, not as a series of codes arising in succession, by a process of historical stratification.

Perhaps the strongest single passage in the Acts is the outline of Stephen's defense which has been given us by Luke in the seventh chapter. We ask our readers to turn to this chapter and read it carefully in the light of modern critical theories. Here the history in which the ritual and legislation are imbedded is given in brief, graphic, and comprehensive form, from Abraham down to the crucifixion of Jesus of Nazareth. The call of Abraham, which some critics explain as a natural migration, the custom of circumcision, which some say was borrowed from the Egyptians, the sojourn and affliction in Egypt, which some critics regard as mythical,. the whole career of Joseph, the life of Moses, and the Exodus under him, are recited with great accuracy in the light of the Pentateuch. The wonders of Sinai, and the giving of the lively oracles there, the incident of the golden calf, a definite allusion to the Tabernacle in the wilderness, made according to the fashion which Moses had seen, the bringing of this Tabernacle, which of course had the complete ritual associated with it, by Joshua into Canaan, the building of the Temple under David and Solomon, and many other particulars, are described in a manner which cannot fail to impress in a peculiar way the reader who may have been perusing some of the radical theories. In particular, verses 44–46 present a view of the Tabernacle and the ritual connected with it in such a way as to make the late origin of the Tabernacle and the so-called Priestly code, impossible, unless we are prepared to set aside the inspired authority of the author of the Acts. Moreover, these verses assume a Mosaic origin for the Tabernacle, and they know nothing whatever about the three codes. So, too, the whole defense made by Stephen lays stress on the era of Moses as the central period of Jewish history and religious interest, and has scarcely anything to say of the days of Josiah and Ezra when the radical critics solemnly inform us that mature Mosaism arose. In a word, almost every feature of radical criticism can be refuted by the wonderful contents of Stephen's remarkable apology. It would be an interesting exercise to attempt to reconstruct this apology in such a way as to bring it into harmony with radical criticism. Such an exercise our readers can follow out for themselves; and we venture the opinion that whoever does this, will be convinced of its absurdity, and be prepared to take his place beside Stephen, Luke, and may we not add, the conservative critics. Moreover, this reconstructed apology would be of no special value for the purpose which Stephen had in view.

In the second place, we may gather some of the teachings of Paul in Romans, Corinthians, and Galatians under a single head, in order to see how Paul can be brought into harmony, if such a thing is possible, with advanced critical conclusions. In Rom. 4 : 1-6, we have significant allusions to Abraham and David, and to the part they played in the Old Testament religion. In Rom. 9 : 4, we have a very important statement about the advantages of the Jews, inasmuch as they had, among other things, "the covenants, and the giving of the law, and the service of God, and the promises." In other parts of the same chapter we have pertinent allusions to Hosea and Isaiah, not easily harmonized with critical views. Chapters 10 and 11 deserve careful study in the same connection, but we cannot refer to particulars in this discussion, which is only too brief.

In 1 Cor. 10 : 1-5, the facts of the Exodus are referred to, and the *spiritual rock*, which was with the people in the Wilderness, is spoken of. In 2 Cor. 3 : 7-15, Paul gives a plain statement concerning the unbelief of the Jews, and connects the whole Old Testament economy with the name of Moses. Surely Paul, an inspired man, had peculiar authority, and his views are to be regarded as of great weight in this debate. And even if we leave out of account the quality of inspiration, we are surely entitled to believe that Paul, who was a thoroughly trained man in the law, knew better what its origin was than any dozen modern critics who cannot even yet agree as to what the assured results of criticism really are.

In Galatians there are one or two passages to which brief reference must now be made. In chapter 3 : 16-29, we have a remarkable exposition of the Mosaic law in relation to Christ, where the law is described as a *pedagogue* to bring us to Christ. According to this passage, the law, evidently regarded as a complete fact, was given four hundred and thirty years after Abraham. This view of the Jews cannot be easily harmonized with the critical view that complete Mosaism did not appear as an actual fact among the people till the age of Ezra. So in chapter 4 : 22-31, we have the allegory of Sarah and Hagar, in which Sinai has prominence in reference to the Old Testament economy as represented by Hagar. We simply ask the radical critics to give an interpretation of this allegory consistent with their theories. The result so far as we can possibly see would be perfectly absurd. For ourselves, we prefer to hold by Paul, even if we thereby incur the charge that our scholarship is quite defective, and that our views are so conservative as to be entirely antiquated, in the judgment of the critics.

In the third place, the Epistle to the Hebrews has great force against radical criticism. It is not necessary to settle the question of the authorship of this epistle, although our own opinion still is that those who deny its Pauline authorship have not yet succeeded in making out their case. In the present discussion all we need to do is to take the epistle as canonical and inspired, and then seek to discover the meaning of its contents in relation to the theories of the Old Testament set forth by radical criticism. The epistle has its well-defined theory of the Mosaic system, and the question is as to its bearing upon the debate between radical and conservative criticism. As this feature of the criticism of radical theories is vitally important, we notice a few points drawn from this epistle.

In the third chapter we have the contrast drawn between Moses and Christ in such a way as to make the former the head of the Old Testament house, as Jesus Christ is of his house. The leadership of Moses in the Exodus is also recognized in this chapter, as also the fatal Wilderness experience of that age. Moses is evidently the historic and legislative center of the Old Testament system as exhibited in this passage.

In chapters 5, 6, 7, we find the case of Melchisedec discussed at length, and in such a way as to confirm the history of Abraham's day and the predictions of David's age. The fourteenth chapter of Genesis, and the one hundred and tenth Psalm should be studied in this connection. In these chapters of Hebrews now under notice also, there is frequent reference to many particulars of the Levitical system, such as the priesthood, the sacrifices, the covenant and its promises, in such a way as to exhibit the view which the writer of this epistle held of the Mosaic system. By him it was clearly held that the Mosaic system was a unit, and that it had all the elements of completeness for its temporary purpose from the beginning. In contrast with Melchisedec we have the Levitical priests of the Aaronic order mentioned in chapter 6: 11, in such a way as to imply the existence of this order, and, of course, of the ritual service with which they were connected, from the time of Aaron. The several orders of the priests are also hinted at.

In chapters 8 and 9, the Tabernacle is described and interpreted in a most interesting and minute way. A whole chapter would be needed to bring out the full force of these chapters against radical criticism. The discussion here naturally connects itself with a former chapter on the Tabernacle of the Old Testament. Here we are told that Moses made the Tabernacle according to the pattern showed him in the Mount. This epistle, therefore, proves the Mosaic genesis of the Tabernacle, and this carries with it the ritual of the Priests' code, especially the solemnities of the Day of Atonement. Then, too, the particulars of the Mosaic system are referred to in these chapters in various ways. The distinction between the clean and unclean, the divers washings, and the carnal ordinances, are mentioned in 9: 10. The fact of a testament, the blood of bulls and of calves, the water, the scarlet wool, and the hyssop, are noted in the same chapter later on, and the meaning of the whole in relation to Christ is explained. The unity and Mosaic origin of the whole scheme which is here described as fulfilled in Christ, are assumed by the author of the epistle. Let the radical critic attempt to reconstruct these two chapters in accordance with his theories, and he will surely be ashamed of the practical application of his theories to this epistle. The author of Hebrews expounding the Tabernacle was evidently not a radical critic.

In the tenth chapter, we have further exposition of the sacrificial system of the religion of Israel, and of the order of priests who officiated under that system. In verse 28, the whole of this system is termed "Moses' law," which surely means that the author of this epistle believed that the entire ritual and legal scheme was Mosaic. If we admit that the author was in error, we seriously impugn the inspiration of that author. Here again we challenge radical criticism to bring this chapter into any sort of harmony with its naturalistic, unhistorical, reconstructive theories. Let the attempt be made, that we may see the form this chapter will take in the revised version which advanced criticism is in duty bound to make.

In the eleventh chapter, we have a record of the heroes of faith given, which, in some respects, resembles the defense of Stephen already alluded to. Here, as in that defense, the history is followed; and as the sketch proceeds, there rise up before us, Abel, Enoch, Noah, Abraham, Isaac, Jacob, Joseph, Moses, and other worthies. Here Abraham and Moses have great prominence given them, while the later history of Israel in those periods when advanced criticism claims that the chief part of the ritual system arose, are passed over with the utmost brevity. The author of the epistle evidently attached far more importance to the hand and age of Moses than the radical critics do. Here reconstruction of the New Testament, in the light of radical theories, would be a tempting task did space permit. It would be an effective *reductio ad absurdum* of radical criticism.

There are other things in the epistle of which we would like to have written; and in other portions of the New Testament there are many things which the radical critics must explain in accordance with their theories of the Old Testament before they have made out their case, but at this point we must close the discussion. The Epistle to the Hebrews especially cannot be expounded by radical criticism.

CHAPTER XVI.

DOCTRINAL CONSIDERATIONS.

AT various stages in our discussions, and especially in the two chapters on the New Testament in its relation to radical criticism, we have seen that the views we are to take of the doctrines of the Christian system are necessarily affected by the conclusions of this school of criticism. In this chapter we proceed to consider this topic a little more fully than we yet have done, so that the general bearing of radical criticism upon some of the essential Christian doctrines may appear. In doing so, we shall be careful to keep in mind that doctrinal or dogmatic views should not alone determine our views in matters of biblical criticism. Exegesis provides the materials for dogmatics. Yet, at the same time, we feel justified in looking at the results of criticism in their relation to well-defined doctrinal conclusions. If in doing so, the result should appear to be that mere theories on the field of criticism are brought into conflict with well-grounded and essential doctrines drawn from the Scriptures, we shall not hesitate to examine these theories with the utmost care. Criticism and dogmatics, therefore, have their mutual relations, and in this chapter we shall be careful to keep these in view, yet not allow doctrine to be dominated by mere critical theory.

In the first place, radical criticism comes into conflict with the doctrine of the unity of the Scriptures of the Old and New Testaments. It has already been pointed out that the organic unity and integrity of the Old Testament is seriously endangered by the methods of literary vivisection which the critics pursue. The point we now further raise has special reference to the New Testament. According to radical criticism, there can be no real bond binding the Old and New Testament Scriptures together. The historical continuity of the stream of revelation is broken, the typical significance of much of the Mosaic system is lost, and the force of the predictive element in prophecy is largely destroyed, if the religion of Israel is merely a natural product of the Semitic genius of the people among whom it originated. The Christian system, together with the literature pertaining to it, is at best a higher stage in the development of religion, and in no proper sense possessed of a supernatural element. There is no spiritual bond to connect the Old and New Testaments, or to link together into an organic whole the books of the New Testament. The whole spirit and methods of advanced criticism look in the direction of destruction and dismemberment, rather than toward construction and unification. The spirit of that one divine life which, we believe, breathes all through the sacred Scriptures, is in great danger of being crushed out by the critical machine.

In the second place, radical criticism demands a recasting of the doctrine of the inspiration of sacred Scripture. As a matter of fact radical criticism often denies inspiration of any kind, and regards the Scriptures as the natural sacred literature of one of the great religions of the world. More moderate critics profess to hold a doctrine of inspiration, but maintain that the old views of that doctrine must be set aside, and a new doctrine which is more in harmony with the results of modern criticism, must be framed. Usually the doctrine is formulated by stating that the people of Israel were under divine guidance, and that in a sense God was present in their national and religious life. Then the Scriptures are held to be the natural product of this inspired people, but as a record they are marked by various human imperfections.

Now, the question we raise against radical criticism here, is this : Is the doctrine of inspiration which it formulates an adequate one ? Does it meet the claim which the Scriptures make concerning their own nature as the word of God ? We think not. For instead of the Scriptures being the natural product of the Jewish nation and Church, that nation and Church were the product of these Scriptures. That the Scriptures could not be the mere natural historical product of the times in which they originated, is proved by the fact that in both the Old and New Testament ages, the contents and teachings of the Scriptures were in advance of their times, and held forth an ideal toward which the people were to strive. Moses and Christ were both in advance of their times, and so their teaching cannot be merely natural wisdom which was the product of the age alone. Then, too, the claims which the authors of the Scriptures make to speak for God, cannot well be harmonized with the views of inspiration which radical criticism tells us must speedily prevail. But we cannot enlarge upon this important point, nor need we do so, for it has already been discussed.

In the third place, according to radical criticism we contend that the doctrine of the Christ of the New Testament, has no real basis in the Old Testament. Even in the Old Testament the continuity of the Messianic promise is broken again and again by the radical theories. In like manner the New Testament fulfillment of that promise is so separated from the Old Testament that the connection is often entirely lost sight of. In like manner the meaning of the Mosaic sacrifices and ritual as typical of Christ is obliterated, and neither the various sacrifices of the Jewish dispensation nor the one sacrifice offered by Christ on the cross, has any redemptive significance in relation to the gracious divine purpose and plan to save sinful men. Christ's person, his offices, and his work have no organic spiritual connection with the Old Testament if the naturalistic conclusions of radical critics are admitted. In this case we shall surely be wise to pause till we see how far the modification of our doctrine of Christ must be made at the behest of the critics. We ought at least to be most careful not to allow radical criticism to rob us of the divine Messiah, who was spoken of by prophet, chanted in praise by psalmist, typified by the Mosaic ritual, and incarnate in the fullness of time. Of him, Moses wrote, to him all the prophets bare witness, and he came to fulfill the law, not to destroy it. With jealous care, therefore, we shall surely guard the honor of our divine Redeemer from the subtle assaults of the relentless critics.

In the fourth place, some of the cardinal doctrines of redemption are seriously affected by the reasonings and conclusions of the radical critics. If the evolutionary view of the Old Testament religion be adopted, then the sacrificial system of that religion was purely natural, and can have no special divine authority. If this be so, we naturally ask on what ground can we hold that Christ died for our sins according to the ' Scriptures? Then, too, if natural development be the true principle according to which the unfolding of the religious knowledge contained in the Old Testament took place, what place can be found for the covenant idea of which so much is said in the Old Testament? This covenant, especially in the form of the evangelical

DOCTRINAL CONSIDERATIONS. 291

covenant, or covenant of grace, implies not simply a natural human development of religion, but a divine gracious purpose to redeem and sanctify sinful men. If, therefore, we destroy the covenant basis of the Old Testament, we certainly affect most seriously the covenant factor in the New.

This is a far-reaching conclusion. It affects the whole question of man's relations to God and the divine law, and it modifies the views we take of the mode of his restoration and recovery from sin. If naturalistic views of the religion of Israel be accepted, then we must reach naturalistic conclusions in regard to the religion of Jesus. According to these naturalistic conclusions, the gospel is no longer a divine remedy for a dreadful malady. Redemption is mere natural improvement of the individual. No objective scheme, with its provisions for reconciliation between God and man, is needed, in fact, none is possible. A simple, natural, subjective experience is all that we require. Hence the whole covenant idea, with its Mediator and mediation, must be set aside, and a simple process of self-conducted moral culture is all that men require to secure salvation.

It is evident also, that the supernatural nature of the experiences involved in regeneration and sanctification is ruled out by radical criticism. Hence not only is the objective reality of the atonement denied, but the supernatural nature of the life of God in the human soul is set aside. In a word, radical criticism affects some of the most essential doctrines of the gospel, both as they relate to the objective facts by which redemption is provided, and as to the subjective experiences by means of which redemption is applied to, and received by, us. Moreover, the view of sin which we must hold is also modified by radical criticism, and the effects of sin upon the race are minimized as much as possible. In a word, radical criticism would introduce confusion into the gospel scheme, and compel such a modification of some of its great doctrines as would make it, indeed, another gospel, which would, as a matter of fact, be no gospel at all.

In the fifth place, no proper place is given for the work of the Holy Spirit by radical criticism. This is true of the religion of Israel, and of the Scriptures of the Old Testament. Natural evolution, not supernatural revelation, is assumed to explain everything here, and so the office of the Holy Spirit is scarcely needed. So in the case of the New Testament the same is true. And even on the experimental side of religion, if natural culture be all that experimental religion implies, then the Holy Spirit to renew and sanctify is not really needed. The consequences of radical criticism at this point are very serious. We frankly confess our inability to see how these results can be brought into harmony with what the Scriptures themselves teach in regard to the work of the Spirit, and concerning the true nature of religious life in the soul. That radical criticism dishonors the Holy Spirit in so evident a manner, is one of the most serious objections which we have to its methods and conclusions on doctrinal grounds.

In closing this chapter it is only proper to remark that what we have said applies especially to radical critical conclusions of naturalistic type. We are well aware, and have been careful not to overlook it in this chapter, that there are critics who pursue the reconstructive methods concerning the Scriptures and the religion they unfold, and who at the same time claim that they do not reject the supernatural nature of this religion. That there are such reverent critics we gladly admit. But at the same time we wish to point out that those who take this position are attempting to stand in very slippery places, and if not extremely careful they may suddenly fall. Many of these men, we believe, are better than the principles they hold in regard to the Scriptures, but the decided tendency will almost surely be to pass more and more into the region of naturalism, if naturalistic methods are adopted. The utmost care should, therefore, be taken at this juncture, for we believe that in the end there will be found no permanent middle ground between thorough-going naturalism and consistent supernaturalism. We close, therefore, with this note of warning regarding the doctrinal dangers of radical criticism.

CHAPTER XVII.

THE EVIDENCE OF ARCHÆOLOGY.

THE last chapter completed our review of doctrinal considerations in relation to the conclusions of radical criticism. In general, it was indicated that the contents of the New Testament, especially the testimony of our Lord and the teachings of the Epistle to the Hebrews, cannot well be harmonized with the views of the Old Testament which radical criticism announces with so much assurance. If Old Testament reconstruction is necessary, equally so is that of the New Testament, and radical critics must not be allowed to overlook this view of the subject.

In this chapter we pass to what might be termed extra-scriptural evidence, and proceed in a very brief way to indicate the force of the results of recent archæological researches in the East in relation to some of the contentions of radical criticism. To a certain extent this is historical testimony at first hand, and, in part, it is monumental evidence of the highest order.

In our present limits it is impossible to give any adequate description of the vast mass of materials which are now at the disposal of scholars in this

THE EVIDENCE OF ARCHÆOLOGY. 295

field. During the past twenty-five or thirty years, excavations have been carried on in the old lands where the events recorded in the Scriptures occurred. In Egypt, in Assyria, and in Babylonia, the old ruins were first made to yield their long-kept secrets. In quite recent years the pick and spade have been busy in Arabia, in Syria, in Phœnicia, and in Palestine, with similar results. By means of these excavations, cylinders with cuneiform writing, tablets with elaborate inscriptions, and stone monuments with engraved characters, have been uncovered in great numbers.

Then a band of noble scholars, with great patience and wonderful skill, have been studying these. In doing so, immense difficulties had to be overcome. To discover the key by which the hieroglyphic and cuneiform writing could be interpreted, was long a difficulty. But the Rosetta Stone, in due time, by means of the Greek, supplied this key. New alphabets had to be formed, but by degrees this was done, and now the deciphering and interpreting of these old records can be effected with comparative ease and accuracy.

Thus the brick cylinders from the mounds of Babylon and Nineveh, the neat tablets found at Tel-el-Amarna, the Moabite stone discovered at Dibhon, and the inscriptions at the pool of Siloam, have spoken to us, and their messages have immense value at the present day in confirming the historicity of the narratives found in the Old Testament, and in enabling us to refute sceptical objections to the sacred Scriptures. Against the advanced theories of radical criticism, the verdict of the monuments is of the highest importance, as we are enabled thereby to test these theories by means of unquestioned extra-scriptural facts. It does seem remarkable that just when such testimony was specially needed, then Providence opened up these old ruins and caused them, after centuries of silent oblivion, to utter their voice in tones so unmistakable as to strike terror into the hosts of the sceptics, and confirm the sometimes wavering faith of the company of believers.

In like manner just when radical criticism was so boldly announcing its attractive theories, the very stones are made to cry out against these baseless speculations. In this chapter we can only point out some of the lines of investigation, and indicate some of the conclusions which support the general views of conservative criticism, based on recent archæological evidence.

In the first place, the mythical view of the contents of the early parts of the Old Testament receives its death blow from the monuments. A century ago, and even less, when there was little evidence beyond the Scriptures to confirm their real historical nature, and when the mythical views of the early classic ages prevailed, the mythical theory of the Old Testament and the early career of Israel had free scope. At least, the materials outside of the Scriptures for its refutation were not at hand, so that it could make unhindered progress.

But the time came, less than fifty years ago, when in classic lands men began to dig in the earth on the supposed sites of ancient cities. Thus ancient Troy was uncovered by Schliemann, and it was shown thereby that Homer's Iliad was not a mere poetic myth. Other classic scenes in Greece, Italy, and Asia Minor were explored, and concrete facts overpowered mythical theories. So in like manner in the lands of Bible story, the same thing has taken place. From Egypt, from Chaldea, from Arabia, and from Palestine, old records of various kinds have been unearthed which forever explode the mythical explanation of the biblical account of the creation, of the deluge, of the exodus, and the wilderness experience of Israel. The Chaldean accounts of the creation and deluge deciphered from the cylinders, and the contents of the Tel-el-Amarna tablets found in Egypt are of special significance in this connection. In the light of these evidences, the mythical theory vanishes away like the morning mist before the rising sun.

In the second place, the evidence of archæology confirms and explains the real historical nature of the biblical narratives at many points. The records from Egypt confirm the Mosaic account of the Exodus; and the Chaldean inscriptions, together with those of Assyria, explain some historical difficulties in Kings and Chronicles, and establish beyond doubt the truth of the biblical history of those periods. Rawlinson and Smith have shown this with great fullness and force. Each succeeding discovery of buried literature only enlarges the confirmation, and there is good reason to expect that when further explorations are made in Arabia and Palestine, where excavations have little more than commenced, additional materials for the explanation and confirmation of biblical history will come to light. The value of such historical and monumental evidence is exceedingly great. It speaks at the present day just as its voice was when first it came into existence, thirty centuries ago. And by its utterances the whole general outline of the history of Israel is confirmed, and so far as the monuments are concerned, no reconstruction such as radical criticism proposes is necessary.

In the third place, we point out the fact that if the general outlines of the history of Israel, as it now stands in the biblical record, be established, then it carries with it the main features of the legislation and ritual as given in the Pentateuch, and as having its existence from the Mosaic era. The testimony of the monuments gives similar prominence to the Mosaic age that the biblical story does, and little confirmation is given to the contention of the radical critics that the period of Ezra was the time of important developments in the religious life of Israel. This really means that the natural evolutionary explanation of this religious life must be abandoned, and the conclusion adopted that that life had its real origin in the age of Moses and in connection with the Exodus, when the ritual and legal scheme was given to the people as the ideal by which they were to frame their national and religious life in Canaan.

In addition, the result of the monumental evidence renders untenable much of the speculations concerning the various literary fragments and various codes supposed to exist in the Scriptures. The origin by piecemeal of the Scriptures is not in harmony with what the inscriptions reveal. If there are various successive strata in the Scriptures, as the critics contend, we would expect to discover some traces of this in the monuments. But such is not the case, as Sayce has so well pointed out.

In the fourth place, the evidence now under notice proves the existence and extensive use of writing at a very early period. This is important in several respects. It has been objected to the Mosaic authorship of the Pentateuch that writing was not practiced to such an extent as to render it possible for Moses to have written the books with which his name has been so closely identified. In like manner, it has been asserted that the main part of the early books of the Old Testament could only have assumed their final literary form in later ages. Radical criticism has not been slow to avail itself of this claim in support of its contention that the religious system of Israel, with the literature which sets it forth, was a gradual growth, and did not assume its mature form and complete contents till long after the time usually ascribed to it. One almost instinctively recalls the fact here that rationalistic scepticism of a century ago, and radical criticism of recent years have virtually joined hands in assailing what are called the *old* views of the Scriptures and the religion of Israel. Strange extremes sometimes meet.

Against this whole line of reasoning, the recent verdict of the tablets and monuments is clear and unmistakable. The cuneiform writing found on the cylinders of Chaldea and Assyria a generation ago gave indications that views formerly held regarding the antiquity of the art of writing would have to be revised. Later discoveries, especially the contents of the tablets found at Tel-el-Amarna in lower Egypt, prove conclusively that writing was known and extensively used at and even prior to the Exodus at the era of Moses. These tablets were, with slight exceptions, written in the Chaldean cuneiform characters, and are so extensive as to form quite a library. From them it is evident that not only were historical and national records kept, but that an extensive correspondence was carried on between Egypt and the East almost a century before the age of Moses and the conquest of Canaan. The names and dates found in these tablets are so definite that there can be no doubt regarding their antiquity, so that their testimony may be regarded as unquestionable. Not only are the contents of the early biblical history confirmed by these inscriptions, but the existence, on an extensive scale, of the art of writing is forever proved. This being the case, one argument against the Mosaic authorship of the early books of the Bible, and in favor of certain factors in the radical critical scheme, is slain and buried out of sight.

In the fifth place, the tablets and inscriptions imply the prevalence, in early times, of a comparatively high degree of literary and intellectual attainment. Their contents justify the conclusion that in Egypt, Chaldea, and in the whole Canaanite region there was a much higher measure of civilization than is often supposed. The contents of the Tel-el-Amarna tablets reveal domestic, legal, commercial, and national transactions which exhibit a complex and somewhat mature civilization of these peoples. Doubtless, as discoveries proceed, further facts will be brought to light to confirm, and perhaps enlarge, this conclusion regarding the early culture of the people associated with the Bible at the beginning of its history. It may be, also, that some of these discoveries may be made in northern Arabia, and in Palestine, where but little has yet been done to bring these hidden literary treasures to light.

The force of this general conclusion regarding early civilization in this region, against certain phases of radical criticism, is evident. When the supporters of this type of criticism, in their advocacy of the natural evolutionary theory of the origin and growth of the nation and religion of Israel, speak of wandering tribes of nomadic habits, and of really no literary culture, or definite monotheistic religious ideas, as constituting the condition of things out of which Israel and its religion came, they are face to face with the contents of the monumental evidence supplied by these recently found tablets. And the testimony of these tablets is against the critics, and condemns the evolutionary theory of the genesis and progress of the religion of Israel at its initial stage. So far as the tablets are concerned, Israel need not have commenced its career in that low degree of literary and religious culture upon which certain critics insist so much.

In closing this chapter, we wish to emphasize the abiding value of this line of research. From various points of view it is useful. It confounds sceptics, and it confirms faith. It explains the Scriptures and expands our views of their contents. It removes seeming inconsistencies in the Scriptures, and sometimes corrects erroneous interpretations into which students may have fallen. In like manner, at the present day, this field of archæology is one of the most important, outside of the Scriptures, wherein we may find materials by which to test and sift the claims and reasonings of modern radical critics. Much has been done already, but much remains still to be done in this field, and we welcome every addition which is made to the already extensive store of facts which have been exhumed. Let the work go on. The greater the light, the clearer the truth will shine, and the more distinctly will the false be exhibited in its true colors.

The value of the testimony which comes from this field consists in the fact that it is extra-scriptural and absolutely unbiased. Having only the contents of the Scriptures to deal with and reason from, there was, of course, difference of opinion without any other witness to give testimony in the case, and there was room for any amount of mere speculation and critical castle-building beyond the contents of the Scriptures. But the monumental evidence comes as an independent witness of probity and impartiality, and its value is of the very highest order.

We rejoice in the work of the Rawlinsons and the Smiths, of the Layards and the Bottas, of the Lenormants and the Navilles, of the Brugschs and the Sayces, of the Petries and the Blisses, of the Pinches and the Schraders, of the Masperos and the Trumbulls. It sheds increasing light on the Scriptures, and really makes the Bible a bigger and a brighter book. It strengthens the defenses round about it, and inspires the faith and courage of its defenders.

This work also gives timely warning to all concerned that the explorations which it makes may spring a mine under some of the leading detachments of radical criticism. The pick and spade of the archæologist may speedily supply a blunt and ready reply to the pen and lance of the radical critic. Some part of this reply has already been given, and we are sure that there is more coming very soon.

CHAPTER XVIII.

SUMMARY.

THROUGH thirty-four chapters we have pursued our discussion concerning Higher Criticism. We have considered especially its advanced, or radical phases. Nearly every aspect of the debate between radical and conservative criticism has been touched upon, although in many cases the treatment was far too meager. In this chapter a general summary may be useful in the way of gathering together the main results which have been attained during the entire discussion.

At the outset of the exposition, several chapters were devoted to a description, or explanation, of biblical criticism, Higher Criticism, and of radical, advanced, or rationalistic criticism, in particular. Here we were careful to point out that Higher Criticism, rightly pursued, is a proper and useful branch of biblical study, and that it was only certain forms of this criticism which were to be subjected to careful scrutiny. These forms are such as pursue their investigation in a purely rationalistic spirit, forgetful of the real nature of the religion and literature represented by the sacred Scriptures.

Against these we feel bound to wage constant warfare in the interests of the truth.

Then several chapters were devoted to a compact history of this phase of literary and historical criticism of the sacred Scriptures, and of the system of ritual and legislation which they unfold. From the days of Porphyry down to the present time, this sketch was pursued. Stress was laid upon the work of Spinoza and Astruc. The development of radical criticism in connection with German rationalism and the Hegelian philosophy was followed out briefly. And, finally, the movements of the present day, in Europe and America, were described. Here, especially, the way in which radical criticism has passed in recent years from Teutonic to Anglo-Saxon circles was pointed out. Moreover, it is worth while noting the fact that in all its earlier stages this type of criticism was made from without the Church, and against the Christian system.

In its later stages, and especially during the present century, this mode of criticism has appeared *within* the Church, and has proceeded to carry on its work within the enclosure of the Christian system. All along we are inclined to think that the history of the radical critical movement is itself a strong argument against it; and its general effects, where it had time to bear its legitimate fruit, constitute its crushing condemnation. Of course, this relates to radical critical methods of Higher Criticism.

When the historical sketch was complete, we proceeded in a somewhat detailed manner to present a statement of the principles and methods assumed and followed by radical critics. Here the underlying philosophical principles were shown to be closely allied with idealistic pantheism, which, of course, excludes the idea of the supernatural. An evolutionary explanation of the origin and growth of religion, and the denial or minimizing of the supernatural in the form of inspiration, naturally followed. That many higher critics of advanced tendencies profess to retain the doctrine of the inspiration of sacred Scripture was also indicated, but that the logic of radical critical methods leads most surely to a denial or ignoring of an inspired and authoritative word of God, such as the Bible claims to be, was also pointed out, partly as a statement of fact, and partly as a warning to those reverent critics who are trying to do what is impossible, in attempting to follow the critical methods of Teutonic rationalism and at the same time maintain the tenets of Anglo-Saxon orthodox doctrine of sacred Scripture.

The exposition next led us to explain a variety of particulars with which Higher Criticism has to deal. The documentary hypothesis of the literature, the theory of the three codes of the religious ritual, the reconstruction of the history, especially at the eras of Moses, Josiah, Ezekiel, and Ezra, the Tabernacle, the graded priesthood, the ritual of the annual feasts, the prophets in their relation to the law, and the contents of the Psalms were the leading particulars which passed under review in a series of successive chapters.

Having completed this statement, we passed on to make a somewhat extended and careful examination of the whole field covered by the exposition and statement referred to above. This criticism, followed in the general lines of the statement made, through several chapters toward the close, dealing with the New Testament in relation to the results of radical criticism, led us on to substantially new ground. No attempt need now be made to summarize that criticism, for it was made in such a condensed manner that it is scarcely possible to make it much more compact.

The remainder of this chapter will be devoted to the mere statement of some of the main conclusions to which our critique of radical criticism has brought us. The following particulars may be noted as conclusions from our discussions : —

First: the philosophy on which radical criticism rests is one which is inimical to Christianity, as a religion having in it a supernatural factor. Whether it be the deistic tendency which renders the supernatural impossible, or the pantheistic tendency which merges the natural and supernatural into one, the results to the Christian system are equally serious. That radical, or rationalistic criticism assumes one or other of these tendencies, we have seen more than once in our discussions. Hence, we signalize its false philosophy, and insist on the vast importance of having a true philosophy of the relation between God and his creatures, and of the essential principles of the divine government in its relation to all forms and classes of beings. To rule out special revelation, and miracle, and a definite providence, by the terms of one's philosophy, is illegitimate, and yet this is just what radical criticism in its general spirit and attitude really does.

Secondly: we have seen reason to conclude that the principle of naturalistic evolution cannot explain the genesis and growth of the religion of Israel, and of Christianity, its goal and fruitage. Indeed, natural evolution alone is inadequate to explain any grade of existence which has in it factors that are not found in the lower grades. Thus the organic cannot come naturally from the inorganic, the conscious from the unconscious, the moral from the non-moral, or the religious from the non-religious. The facts support this view, and the law of causation confirms it, for an adequate cause of the new factor in the higher form of existence is required. So in regard to religion and its development, as seen in the Old and New Testaments. The law of natural evolution is degeneration, and the adequate cause of the advance in religious thought and life seen in the Scriptures is the divine agency working in a supernatural way, in chosen men, during successive ages. This is the true view of the philosophy of religion, and it condemns radical criticism at its very outset.

Thirdly: the whole analysis of the documents of which the Scriptures are supposed to have been composed, and the division into separate codes to which the Mosaic system is subjected, have been seen in several respects to be forced and unnatural. As this is a cardinal point in radical criticism, it is worth while emphasizing it. There is so much assumption, and so many suppositions made, and, at present, so little harmony of view among the critics that no "assured results of criticism" are yet in sight. Moreover, it seems that having assumed three codes, the literature must be made to fit this assumption, or having assumed a diversity of documents, a codification of the ritual became necessary. In either case, the method of procedure is gratuitous, for the simple view is to assume neither distinct documents nor successive codes and everything remains simple, natural, and clear.

Fourthly: we have seen frequent reason to conclude that radical criticism is condemned on historical grounds. This is virtually conceded by the critics themselves when they assume that the biblical history must be reconstructed. The proposed reconstruction is required because the theory demands it, not because historical evidence makes it necessary. The result of this reconstruction of the history is virtually its inversion. Instead of mature

Mosaism being the ideal before the people from the first, it was the stage last reached. The prophets were before the law, the Temple prior to the idea of the Tabernacle, the kingdom before any directions about the king and the manner of the kingdom. Then, too, the absurdity of an attempt to reconstruct the history without any requisite materials, but in an ideal way, is written on its very face. It is the old and useless attempt of a man trying to transport himself over a high fence by lifting up his feet in his hands.

Fifthly: if the historicity of the Old Testament narratives be made out, as we believe it may be, against radical criticism, then many important positions of that criticism are refuted. Our discussion has enabled us to see several of these. It has shown that the religious life and sentiment of the age of Moses, of David, and of the early prophets, was such as to render it possible for the religious teaching of these persons to have been suitable for these ages; it has shown that silence concerning the observance of the ritual in any given age does not prove its non-existence in that age; it has shown that from the first the complete Mosaic system was the ideal before the people, but that oftentimes they came short of that legal and ritual ideal and were punished for defection; and it has shown that the predictive element in prophecy has reality. These are some of the main positions of radical criticism which the vindication of the history refutes. The importance of the historical, as distinguished from the purely linguistic line of criticism, is also illustrated at this point.

Sixthly: the silent but eloquent testimony of the monuments constitute one of the most interesting and valuable lines of study for the refutation of radical criticism which is at our disposal at the present day. The burden of this testimony goes to show that the critics are at least unhistorical in their procedure.

Lastly: it has appeared that the organic connection between the Old Testament and the New, is a topic to which radical criticism has not given sufficient attention. Perhaps their omission to discuss this point at length, was dictated by prudential considerations, for we believe that in this connection one of the very great weaknesses of radical criticism will appear. In all biblical studies, and all expositions of the Christian system, both Testaments must be taken into account. The religion of Israel does not stand by itself, nor does the Christian system. Both are included under the view we should take of the Christian system as the religion of the Bible. This being the case, radical criticism of the Old Testament must be estimated in part, at least, from its relation to the New Testament. In our discussions we have seen how weak radical criticism is at this point. The New Testament history, the prophetic fulfillment it gives, the doctrinal and redemptive scheme it founds on the Old Testament, and, above all, the direct and indirect teaching of our Lord interpreting the law and the prophets, are all arranged in solid phalanx against radical criticism. To be consistent on New Testament ground, radical criticism must proceed to reconstruct it just as they attempt to reconstruct the Old Testament. We shall not be surprised if the next move of radical criticism is in this direction. When this is done, its work will be complete, and its doom will be forever sealed. We wait and watch meantime.

CHAPTER XIX.

CONCLUDING REMARKS.

WE are now in sight of the end of our long journey. In this concluding chapter, we shall present a few general reflections, with which our discussions of radical criticism may fittingly conclude. These reflections must be quite general in their nature, and will relate chiefly to the spirit and attitude of conservative criticism at this juncture, and to the prospective outcome of the present debate between it and radical criticism.

In the first place, we repeat what has been said more than once, that the Higher Criticism is a legitimate and useful branch of biblical study. It is not only proper, but necessary, that the topics embraced under this study should be investigated by the biblical scholar. We insist that the conservative critic has a perfect right to this field, and the tacit assumption that the radical critic is the only scholar competent to handle aright the topics which pertain to the Higher Criticism is one which, in the interests of true critical investigation, we ought by no means to allow. All the questions of authorship, literary features, and mode of composition of the sacred Scriptures; all debate as to the origin and growth of the religion of Israel, and the nature of the Mosaic system, together with all related historical inquiries, are matters which, from the conservative standpoint, not only should the biblical scholar feel free to investigate, but he should also feel that it is his duty faithfully to canvass this whole field.

In the second place, we cannot refrain from uttering a protest against the arrogant claims which the radical critics so often make for a monopoly of competent scholarship in this field. Indeed, the situation at this point would be quite amusing, if it had not also its serious side. Here are the radical critics, and a great, learned, and reverent company they are. The world had never before beheld their equal, and may never see their like again. They seem to know more about what took place in the days of Moses, of David, of Josiah, and of Ezra, than the persons who lived at or near the time of these men. And yet so wonderful is the result of this remarkable modern scholarship that no two of its chief leaders are entirely agreed as to the main positions to be held and taught, as settled forever beyond dispute. Now, we ask, what advantage in ability, in culture, in spiritual insight, and in logical acumen, can these radical critics possibly possess? For our own part, it does seem to be very often the ability to pull down and destroy that they chiefly exhibit, and this is not necessarily a high order of ability. A very stupid man may deny anything, and hold to his denial with tenacity; and a man of little brains, and less sense, can raise objections to any well-established truth. We can see nothing in the work which radical criticism is doing which argues the necessary possession of ability and scholarship far in advance of the more sober or conservative critics. It is not so much a question of gifts and culture, as of standpoint and method that is here involved, and from this view-point the conservative has, as we think, the decided advantage in the discussion.

In the third place, we make a remark on the present status of radical criticism. No extensive review of the situation is here possible, but a few simple things deserve notice. In Germany, where less than a generation ago, modern radical theories were born and cradled in the nursery of the Hegelian philosophy, there has appeared, in recent years, a decided reaction against extremely radical conclusions. There is, at the present time, a sort of civil war going on among the critics in the German universities, and during the last two or three years the *ultra* radical school has had decidedly the worst of it. The people, and the university authorities, are also protesting against the evils of rationalistic criticism. In Britain matters are apparently in the balance. Some seem to be tired of wearing the second-hand clothes of German professors; and in Scotland, the latest importation in the person of **Professor Pfleiderer, of Berlin, to give the Gifford**

Lectures in Glasgow, turned out so badly as to call for a defense of sound Christian doctrine at the hands of three Scottish professors. This, we trust, will prove a healthy lesson. In England, the critics, especially Driver and Cheyne, are fully agreed upon little else than a common antagonism to what they term *traditional* views. In America, we are in the thick of the fray yet, with here and there signs that the tide is turning against the radical conclusions. The result in certain recent judicial cases, and the excellent writings of the conservatives, have had a decided effect, and may do something to check its spread. Still we are inclined to think that it will run its course here, as elsewhere, and we doubt whether we have seen the end of its career yet on this continent.

In the fourth place, as to the final outcome of the whole critical movement, a word or two should be spoken. Some on the side of orthodox doctrinal truth are inclined to take a gloomy view of the situation, and seem to think that the case for the conservatives is almost hopeless. The boasts of the radicals are suited to this frame of mind, and may have had something to do with producing it. Certainly, this hopelessness of some conservatives is a spirit which is very pleasing to the radicals, and cannot fail to cheer them on to supposed victory. But over against this gloomy view we do not hesitate to cherish a bright and hopeful attitude. In the past, again and again, good men have trembled for the ark of God when it has been assailed, but just as often have we seen it pass through the conflict unharmed, and perhaps all the stronger because of the conflict safely endured. So we are convinced it will be in this case. After the stress to which conservative views on biblical questions are now put by radical criticism, is over, we are sure that if past history means anything, and if Christianity still has its divine vitality, as we believe it has, it will turn out that the Bible is more firmly entrenched as the word of God than ever. There is work, much work, for every lover of sound views on Scripture truth and the doctrines of the gospel, to do; but this work may be conducted in a patient, scholarly temper of mind, and with a hopefulness of spirit which will ensure success in the end. And all the while we may remember that only what costs much is after all worth much.

In the fifth place, we wish to insist on what we believe to be equally true in this connection. We are fully convinced that the spirit, methods, principles, and conclusions of radical criticism are exceedingly dangerous to evangelical truth. Our conviction is that if the general conclusions of radical criticism in regard to the origin, growth, and nature of the religion of Israel, and in regard to the presence of the supernatural in the entire Scriptures be adopted, it would be necessary to so reconstruct the main contents of the Christian system as to entirely change its whole scope. The contention, therefore, that the critic may pursue his critical methods without reference to the relation which these methods have to the doctrinal system imbedded in Scripture, is not sound in itself considered, and is an exceedingly dangerous one in its practical applications. The fact, too, that the processes of the radical critics go far deeper than what may be termed the surface questions of a literary and linguistic nature, adds further force to this consideration. If we admit the radical critical view, in regard to the natural evolutionary nature of the Old Testament religion, it will not be possible to hold supernatural views of the New. It is, in our judgment, a matter of life and death for evangelical Christian truth and life to determine whether radical critical conclusions shall be admitted or refuted. Let no one think lightly of the issues involved, and let none be discouraged in the conflict. The truth, even if at times crushed to earth, shall rise again.

In the sixth place, an interesting question arises when we seek to determine how far these radical critical conclusions can be held in harmony with a sincere and unreserved subscription to the standards of the Presbyterian Church. In cases of judicial process for heresy respecting these views, this question at once becomes an exceedingly difficult and practical one. That a man may pursue the inquiries to which Higher Criticism addresses itself, is freely admitted, so that in itself considered, Higher Criticism conducted in a proper way is not inconsistent with the loyal acceptance of our creed symbols. But if this criticism proceeds upon false principles, and according to erroneous methods, then its conclusions may be contra-confessional, and so be such as to justly call for inquiry by the Church Court. Further, we believe that radical criticism and its naturalistic conclusions are incapable of being harmonized with our standards. The doctrine of Holy Scripture, the sinful state of man, the covenant plan of grace, the essential nature of the work of Christ, and the spiritual renovation which man needs, are all points where conflict must arise. In addition, the whole tone and temper of radical criticism — in a word, its general spirit — is not in tune with the views of gospel truth unfolded in the confession and catechisms. There are therefore limits to legitimate criticism, as there are also to sound exegesis. Radical criticism in our judgment transgresses these limits, and conservative criticism should be careful to keep within the proper bounds, which are necessarily set by the nature of the Christian system.

We conclude this chapter and close the entire series with a simple practical challenge. Last year, during the session of Louisville Presbyterian Theological Seminary, the annual Catalogue or Announcement, as is usual in such institutions, was issued. In compiling this little pamphlet each of the six members of the faculty had a share. The brief statement concerning each school was drawn up by the professor in charge of that school. Some introductory explanations were taken, with several changes and additions, from a brief Announcement issued a year ago. One of the professors drew up some brief remarks in regard to the general working of the seminary, the clerk of the faculty supplied the roll of students from his book, and the librarian handed in his article upon that topic.

Then a committee of two, appointed by the faculty, took all this undigested material thus provided, and sought to reduce it to an orderly, harmonious whole. Some of the statements given by the professors were published almost without change, others were modified, and one or two were almost entirely recast in order to reduce all to symmetrical form. Then the president of the board of directors revised the whole, suggesting some changes which were adopted by the committee. Then, after the matter was set up in *proof* by the printers, some further changes were made in proof-reading, until, after all these revisions or redactions, it came forth in its complete form. Now, we are prepared to submit this little publication of thirty odd pages to a committee of radical critics chosen from the whole world of modern scholarship, and challenge them to make an analysis of these pages in such a way as to show how much of their contents is due to the several professors, how much to the redaction of the committee who had its publication in charge, and how much is due to the hand of the president of the board. We will give the committee of the radical critics a year to bring in their report, and it needs no prophet to say that the report will be wide of the mark, if they should be bold enough to make any at all.

If, in such a small matter, not yet a year old, it is virtually impossible to trace the work of the different hands which helped to produce it, how infinitely more difficult is the task which radical criticism undertakes when it makes the attempt to analyze the Old Testament Scriptures, and label each portion with some symbol to denote its age and authorship. Even if the Scriptures were composed as the radical critics argue, it is impossible now to make the analysis, and the critics who try it are simply building castles in the air. Till a simple challenge, like the one above issued, is successfully answered, the right and ability of the critics to present an assured analysis of the Old Testament cannot be allowed. Their professed schemes are simply impositions which only a hasty credulity is likely to accept.

In closing, we add that we gladly welcome every legitimate attempt to understand more fully the sacred Scriptures of the Christian system. Even if the present critical movement seems at times to threaten serious harm to evangelical faith, yet we feel sure that the divine Hand who first gave the

Scriptures will preserve them in all these fires of criticism, and bring them forth as gold tried by the fire. Nor have we any desire to remove the Scriptures from the most rigid scrutiny, for we are satisfied that the more the Bible is inspected the more fully its divine credentials will appear, and the more it is exposed to the friction of even unfriendly criticism, the more brightly it will shine in its own pure and native luster.

We are also equally sure that no naturalistic view of the gospel scheme will long meet and satisfy the urgent needs of sinful, burdened, struggling men, or permanently enable the pulpit to maintain its rightful preëminence. Any critical conclusions which tend to naturalism, or to dishonor the word and Spirit of God, are fraught with danger. What this age, and every age, needs is not naturalistic nostrums for evils which only a divine remedy can heal; and every pulpit in the land should be, not a platform where *dilettante* essays on almost every theme save the gospel are delivered for the entertainment of the hearers, but a sacred place where the gospel of the grace of God is earnestly, lovingly, and faithfully declared for the salvation of sinful men.

www.ingramcontent.com/pod-product-compliance
Lightning Source LLC
Chambersburg PA
CBHW030748230426
43667CB00007B/886